ISBN 0 11 322002 2

National Heart Forum

Tavistock House South

Tavistock Square

London WC1H 9LG

Registered Company Number: 2487644

Registered Charity Number: 803286

VAT Number: 564 6088 18

Other publications by the National Heart Forum:

Coronary Heart Disease Prevention in Undergraduate Medical Education
Coronary Heart Disease Prevention: A Catalogue of Key Resources
Coronary Heart Disease Prevention: Action in the UK 1984–1987
Coronary Heart Disease: Are Women Special?
Eat Your Words: Understanding Healthy Eating and Food Messages
Food For Children: Influencing Choice and Investing in Health
Physical Activity: An Agenda for Action
Preventing Coronary Heart Disease in Primary Care: The Way Forward
Preventing Coronary Heart Disease: The Role of Antioxidants, Vegetables and Fruit
School Meals Assessment Pack

Published by The Stationery Office and available from:

The Publications Centre
(mail, telephone and fax orders only)
PO Box 276, London SW8 5DT
General enquiries 0171 873 0011
Telephone orders 0171 873 9090
Fax orders 0171 873 8200

The Stationery Office Bookshops
49 High Holborn, London WC1V 6HB
(counter service and fax orders only)
Fax 0171 831 1326
68-69 Bull Street, Birmingham B4 6AD
0121 236 9696 Fax 0121 236 9699
33 Wine Street, Bristol BS1 2BQ
0117 926 4306 Fax 0117 929 4515
9-21 Princess Street, Manchester M60 8AS
0161 834 7201 Fax 0161 833 0634
16 Arthur Street, Belfast BT1 4GD
01232 238451 Fax 01232 235401
The Stationery Office Oriel Bookshop
The Friary, Cardiff CF1 4AA
01222 395548 Fax 01222 384347
71 Lothian Road, Edinburgh EH3 9AZ
(counter service only)

Customers in Scotland may
mail, telephone or fax their orders to:
Scottish Publications Sales
South Gyle Crescent, Edinburgh EH12 9EB
0131 479 3141 Fax 0131 479 3142

Accredited Agents
(see Yellow Pages)

and through good booksellers

At Least Five a Day

Strategies to increase vegetable and fruit consumption

Edited by Imogen Sharp

National Heart Forum
Tavistock House South
Tavistock Square
London WC1H 9LG

London: The Stationery Office

Acknowledgements

This report is based on a one-day expert meeting on *Strategies to Increase Fruit and Vegetable Consumption*, held in April 1996. The National Heart Forum would like to thank all those who helped to organise and all those who participated in the meeting. Particular thanks are due to:

- The Steering Group:
  Dr Fleur Fisher, British Medical Association (Chair of Steering Group)
  Mr Geoffrey Cannon, National Food Alliance and World Cancer Research Fund
  Ms Anne Dillon Roberts, formerly National Farmers Union
  Ms Ann Foster, Scottish Consumer Council
  Mr Trevor Hayes, National Farmers Union
  Professor Desmond Julian, Chairman, National Heart Forum
  Professor Tim Lang, National Food Alliance
  Professor Michael Marmot, University College London
  Dr Alan Maryon Davis, Faculty of Public Health Medicine
  Professor Michael Oliver, National Heart and Lung Institute
  Professor Brian Pentecost, British Heart Foundation
  Dr Lesley Rogers, National Heart Forum
  Ms Maggie Sanderson, British Dietetic Association
  Ms Imogen Sharp, Director, National Heart Forum
  Ms Lynn Stockley, Health Education Authority
  Ms Carmen Taboas, National Consumer Council
  Ms Carol Williams, Nutrition consultant
  Dr Martin Wiseman, Department of Health
  Dr John Yarnell, Health Promotion Agency for Northern Ireland

- All the speakers who contributed papers, the session chairs, and all the other participants who contributed to the success of the expert meeting

- The Health Education Authority, the World Cancer Research Fund, and the National Farmers Union for funding the expert meeting and report

- Karen McColl and Rosie Leyden for editorial work on the report

- The meeting coordinators, Dr Lesley Rogers and Ms Jenni White, National Heart Forum

- The British Heart Foundation for permission to reproduce the graphics used in Figures 1–7 in Chapter 1, from their publication *Coronary Heart Disease Statistics: Diet and Nutrition Supplement* (1996).

National Heart Forum

The National Heart Forum (formerly the National Forum for Coronary Heart Disease Prevention) is an alliance of over 35 national organisations concerned with the prevention of coronary heart disease. Members represent the health services, professional bodies, consumer groups and voluntary organisations.

The mission of the National Heart Forum is to work with and through its members to achieve a reduction in coronary heart disease mortality and morbidity rates throughout the UK. It has four main objectives:

- to keep under review the activities of member organisations and disseminate findings

- to identify areas of consensus, issues of controversy, and needs for action

- to facilitate the coordination of activities between interested organisations

- to make recommendations where appropriate.

Member organisations
ASH (Action on Smoking and Health)
Association for Public Health
Association of Facilitators in Primary Care
British Association for Cardiac Rehabilitation
British Cardiac Society
British Dietetic Association
British Heart Foundation
British Medical Association
British Nutrition Foundation
Chartered Institute of Environmental Health
Consumers' Association
CORDA
Coronary Prevention Group
Faculty of Public Health Medicine
Family Heart Association
Health Education Authority
Health Promotion Agency for Northern Ireland
Health Promotion Wales
Health Visitors' Association
National Association of Governors and Managers
National Association of Health Authorities and Trusts
Northern Ireland Chest, Heart and Stroke Association
Royal College of General Practitioners
Royal College of Nursing
Royal College of Paediatrics and Child Health

Royal College of Physicians of Edinburgh
Royal College of Physicians of London
Royal College of Surgeons of England
Royal Institute of Public Health and Hygiene
Royal Pharmaceutical Society of Great Britain
Society of Cardiothoracic Surgeons
Society of Health Education and Health Promotion Specialists
Society of Occupational Medicine
Sports Council
Trades Union Congress

Observers
Department of Health
Department of Health and Social Services, Northern Ireland
Medical Research Council
Ministry of Agriculture, Fisheries and Food
National Consumer Council
Scottish Consumer Council
Scottish Office, Home and Health Department
Welsh Office

In addition, a number of distinguished experts in the field have individual membership.

Contents

Foreword

It has long been recognised that vegetables and fruit are beneficial for health. The current interest in fruit and vegetables, and the national and international recommendations to eat at least five portions a day, stem largely from research on the role of antioxidant nutrients in preventing chronic diseases such as coronary heart disease and some cancers.

The UK population currently eats an average of three portions of fruit and vegetables each day. This report sets out strategies for achieving the goal of at least five portions a day. It derives from an expert meeting held by the National Heart Forum in 1996, which brought together almost 90 participants from the wide range of agencies involved in the production, provision and promotion of fruit and vegetables. It builds on *Preventing Coronary Heart Disease: The Role of Antioxidants, Vegetables and Fruit*,[1] an earlier Forum initiative.

The aim of this National Heart Forum initiative is to contribute to an increase in fruit and vegetable consumption in the UK, by examining current trends in consumption; exploring opportunities and barriers to achieving the goal of at least five portions a day; identifying options and practical strategies for different sectors; and stimulating action.

In the case of vegetables and fruits, what is good for health is also good for business. Achieving an increase in the consumption of fruit and vegetables will be good for farmers and good for retailers, as well as good for consumers. The enthusiasm and support for action to increase vegetable and fruit consumption was evident across the many sectors represented at the National Heart Forum meeting, with clear consensus that the time is ripe for change. The recommendations that emerged had considerable support from the large majority of participants.

International experience shows that interventions to increase vegetable and fruit consumption can work, but the lessons are that messages need to be clear, simple and consistent, and that coordinated and sustained action across different sectors is needed. The national health strategies in the UK, and their action plans, provide an important policy context for change, although, as they have already recognised, achieving long-term change is not an easy task.

Throughout this report, 'vegetables and fruit' is used interchangeably with 'fruit and vegetables'. Although the term 'fruit and vegetables' is more familiar, 'vegetables and fruit' has been used in order to provoke thought and action, since it is clear that unless people eat more vegetables as well as more fruit, they are unlikely to achieve the goal of 'at least five a day'.

We are grateful to the Health Education Authority, the National Farmers Union and the World Cancer Research Fund for providing funding assistance for this initiative. We hope that it will stimulate action to increase vegetable and fruit consumption in the UK so that the goal of 'at least five a day' becomes a reality.

Professor Desmond Julian CBE MD FRCP
Chairman, National Heart Forum

Reference

1   National Heart Forum. 1997. *Preventing Coronary Heart Disease: The Role of Antioxidants, Vegetables and Fruit.* London: The Stationery Office.

Part 1

The way forward: summary and recommendations

Throughout this report 'vegetables and fruit' is used interchangeably with 'fruit and vegetables'. Although the term 'fruit and vegetables' is more familiar, 'vegetables and fruit' has been used in order to provoke thought and action. Vegetables have traditionally been regarded as 'filler foods' and relatively uninteresting. The new emphasis on vegetables and fruit in strategies to protect against chronic diseases such as coronary heart disease and some cancers, and the need to change the UK diet, demand a new focus. It is clear that unless people eat more vegetables as well as more fruit, they are unlikely to achieve the goal of 'at least five a day'.

The way forward: summary and recommendations

There has been increasing attention in the early 1990s on the health benefits of fruit and vegetables and, in particular, of their antioxidant properties. There is evidence that high consumption of vegetables and fruit can help protect against coronary heart disease and some cancers. The National Heart Forum considered the scientific evidence relating to vegetables and fruit and antioxidant nutrients at an expert meeting in March 1995 and reached the following consensus, which is set out in the report *Preventing Coronary Heart Disease: The Role of Antioxidants, Vegetables and Fruit.*[1]

- There is good evidence that a diet rich in a range of vegetables and fruit is beneficial and lowers the risk of coronary heart disease.

- National and international recommendations to increase fruit and vegetable intakes to at least five portions a day form a sound basis for policy.

- Evidence for a protective effect of specific antioxidants, particularly vitamins E and C and beta-carotene, is incomplete; further research is needed before recommendations for specific antioxidants can be made.

The healthy eating message in relation to fruit and vegetables has remained remarkably consistent over time, although the rationale has changed. Recent reports, including those from the World Health Organization[2] and the Committee on Medical Aspects of Food Policy[3] as well as *The Scottish Diet*[4] report, support the need for an increase in vegetable and fruit consumption. This has been translated into advice for the general public to eat at least five portions of fruit and vegetables a day, which is equivalent to a daily intake of around 400g per person.

There is still a gap between recommended and actual levels of consumption of fruit and vegetables in the UK. The average intake is estimated to be around 250g per person per day – roughly equivalent to three portions each day. Some groups are closer to the target than others. Older people, for example, eat more fruit and vegetables than younger people. People in lower socioeconomic groups are further from the target than those in higher socioeconomic groups. There are also differences between regions.

Barriers to increasing fruit and vegetable consumption

Many barriers prevent people from attaining the 'at least five a day' goal. Although attention has traditionally focused on barriers operating at the individual level, many of the barriers are systemic – operating throughout society and at all stages in the food chain. The solutions will depend on the commitment of a wide range of agencies, in particular the food industry (producers, manufacturers, retailers and caterers) and the government.

The barriers to increasing fruit and vegetable consumption fall into two general types:

- availability of and access to fruit and vegetables, and

- individual attitudes to and knowledge about fruit and vegetables, and trends in eating patterns.

The problems of availability and access are due partly to changes in food retailing and partly to social and demographic changes. The concentration of food retailing has resulted in fewer, larger stores, often out of town. This has created some areas where there is no longer ready access to a wide choice of affordable foods, particularly vegetables and fruit. The fruit and vegetables which people in these areas can buy locally tend to be more expensive and of poorer quality.

Demographic changes which are relevant include the increase in single-person households, an ageing and less mobile population, and concentrations of unemployment in particular areas. Working patterns, changes in car ownership, shopping patterns and advancing technology have also had an impact on eating patterns. Partly as a consequence of these changes, British eating habits have changed, squeezing vegetables and fruit out of daily life. The traditional sit-down meal – often seen as the 'vegetable slot', offering the opportunity for one or two portions – is disappearing in favour of convenience foods and solitary snacking.

People's attitudes to vegetables and fruit also have an important effect on consumption levels. Vegetables are often seen as boring, unappetising and inconvenient, and fruit as expensive. Limited knowledge of how to serve vegetables and the fact that children often dislike them are further reasons for their unpopularity. Fruit and salad are not thought to be filling enough. In general, there is low awareness of the specific health benefits of vegetables and fruit. While people are aware that fruit and vegetables are 'good for you' they are unaware of the specific diet-disease relationships. Furthermore, many people think that they already eat enough vegetables and fruit – even though they are not reaching the 'at least five a day' goal.

Coordinated action

There is a need to devise ways of fitting vegetables and fruit into modern lifestyles. Strategies need to focus on ways to structure the opportunities for eating vegetables and fruit into daily eating patterns, and will need to look wider than health education. In other words, a strategy should include ways of improving availability of and access to fruit and vegetables as well as changing attitudes, and it needs to be backed by political will. It is encouraging to see the successes of strategies to increase fruit and vegetable consumption in other countries. The national health strategies in England, Scotland, Northern Ireland and Wales and their action plans provide a useful framework. Consideration was given to many of these issues, and how to carry them forward, by the Nutrition Task Force and by the Scottish Diet Action Group (see Chapter 4). It is clear that achieving coordinated action and bringing about long-term change is not without problems.

There was much enthusiasm and support at the National Heart Forum expert meeting – across the wide range of sectors represented – for a coordinated strategy and campaign to increase vegetable and fruit consumption. It would be in everyone's interests and would be a boost for business. Increasing vegetable and fruit consumption in the UK would be good for farmers and growers, good for retailers and good for the health of consumers. The expert meeting reached a broad consensus and the following recommendations emerged. They had considerable support from the large majority of participants.

1 A national coordinated and sustained strategy to increase fruit and vegetable consumption, involving the food industry and government as well as health and consumer groups, is urgently needed.

Coordination is needed at a national level, with appropriate resources, to ensure a sustained strategy with a clear and consistent message. Such a strategy should tackle availability and access to vegetables and fruit as well as changing attitudes and awareness. The strategy would need to include a high profile information campaign and be supported by structural change and local action.

Experience overseas has shown that a broad-ranging, multi-sectoral strategy to promote fruit and vegetables is required to achieve results. In the United States, for example, the national *5 A Day* programme has successfully developed private/public partnerships across all 50 states involving health departments, the food industry and the mass media (see Chapter 8).

Many players should be involved in the strategy, which would require strong leadership and coordination. There is a need for government, all sections of the food industry (producers, processors, manufacturers, retailers and caterers), health professionals, local authorities, schools, researchers, the media, the voluntary sector and consumer groups, to be involved in developing and implementing the strategy.

One option is for a national coalition, funded by government, industry and other stakeholders such as health groups. Local action, however, will also be important and local alliances will be needed. Research in the UK shows that practical interventions can be effective in increasing fruit and vegetable consumption towards the 'at least five a day' goal (see Chapter 7).

Any strategy will need to take into account the economic effects of an increase in vegetable and fruit consumption, such as the effect on the balance of trade in terms of imports and exports. The environmental effects of increasing consumption will also need to be considered.

2   Agencies promoting vegetables and fruit should give a clear, simple and consistent message to eat 'at least five a day'.

It is important that all agencies, from health professionals to the food industry, give the same message about vegetables and fruit. This message must be clear and simple. Organisations should find meaningful and appealing ways of getting the message across. Research has shown that quantified advice for the public – such as specifying the number of portions of vegetables and fruit to aim for, rather than simply 'eat more' or 'double' – is particularly useful. It is also important that the vegetable and fruit message remains consistent and is not tainted by the perception that healthy eating messages change so much that they cannot be credible.

It is important to be clear what is meant by 'vegetables and fruit'. The 'at least five a day' message includes different types of fruit and vegetables – fresh, frozen and processed (see Chapter 1). Some type of guidance on what is included within the definition of vegetables and fruit and, where appropriate, on what constitutes a portion would be useful. Guidelines on how to promote the fruit and vegetable message to different groups could be useful in clarifying these issues.

3   Targeted strategies to increase vegetable and fruit consumption are needed, with a particular focus on children, low income groups and regions with low consumption.

There are marked differences in fruit and vegetable consumption levels by age. Younger people eat less, with two thirds (66%) of 16-24 year olds consuming fruit less than once a day and 48% consuming vegetables or salad less than once a day. Research shows that childhood fruit and vegetable consumption is a strong predictor of adult consumption. It is therefore vital that children are a priority in any strategy to increase fruit and vegetable consumption.

Lower income groups tend to have much lower intakes of fruit and vegetables. People in socioeconomic groups IV and V, for example, would need to double their vegetable and fruit consumption (a 100% increase) to reach the goal of 400g a day. An increase of only 30% would be needed by socioeconomic groups I and II. There are also variations by region. Scotland, for example, has particularly low levels of fruit and vegetable consumption. Targeting these groups is particularly important because populations on low incomes, and those in regions with low fruit and vegetable consumption, also have the highest rates of coronary heart disease (see Chapter 1).

Research has shown that targeted approaches are successful in encouraging fruit and vegetable consumption. Strategies should be tailored according to how much fruit and vegetables people are already eating, their attitudes to fruit and vegetables, and how much access they have to them.

4   **There is an urgent need for a national, high profile information and education campaign to improve the image of vegetables and fruit and re-position them as appealing and appetising.**

Research has shown that few people are aware of the 'at least five a day' message and that many people think that their diets are healthier than they actually are. Many people, for example, consider that their diets are healthy because they eat 'some' fruit and vegetables. Furthermore, vegetables are often thought of as boring, unappetising and difficult to prepare, and fruit is perceived as costly.

If vegetable and fruit consumption is to be increased, there is, therefore, a need for a high profile information campaign which improves the image of vegetables and fruit, corrects people's misperceptions about their own diets and also raises awareness of the health message. Such a campaign must be set within the context of a wider strategy and supported by national and local policies (see Recommendation 1).

Campaigns should take on board lessons from other countries and other campaigns. Research into the *5 A Day* programme in the United States suggests a high awareness of the '5 A Day' message and that those people who were aware of the message were more likely to eat more fruit and vegetables. In Victoria, Australia, results from the *2 Fruit 'n' 5 Veg Every Day* campaign suggest that the number of people eating more than five servings of vegetables a day has increased since the campaign began.

European Union

5   **The reformed fruit and vegetables regime of the Common Agricultural Policy should be implemented in the UK in such a way as to increase vegetable and fruit consumption.**

The production support mechanisms of the Common Agricultural Policy (CAP) have acted as a barrier between producers and consumers to some degree. This has hindered growers in responding quickly to changing consumer demands and resulted in some distortions in the pricing and supply of fruit and vegetables. As with other agricultural produce, the CAP has resulted in consumers paying artificially high prices for fruit and vegetables. The fruit and vegetables regime alone cost 1.5 billion ecus (approximately £1.83 billion) in 1994. There has also been an enormous amount of wastage under the CAP with huge quantities of produce withdrawn from the market and usually destroyed or fed to animals, amounting to 45% of the cost of the regime. Furthermore, good quality produce was withdrawn while sub-standard produce remained on the market (see Chapter 3).

The 1996 reforms of the fruit and vegetables regime present an opportunity for the fruit and vegetable sector to become more market oriented. This will depend on the priorities of producer organisations, which have been given more powers in the reformed regime. The potential size and monopoly power of the producer organisations are of concern to the UK fruit and vegetable sector as well as to consumer groups. Producer organisations should focus their activities on promoting fruit and vegetable varieties with the aim of increasing consumer demand for domestic produce. Although problems of spoilage and transport costs have to be considered, mechanisms of distributing remaining surplus fruit and vegetables should be explored and encouraged, such as free or subsidised distribution to schools or nurseries. Grading and quality requirements also need to be reviewed so that they do not prevent smaller and cheaper products from reaching the market, such as small apples for children.

It is important, however, that the fruit and vegetables regime of the CAP is not considered in isolation. The effect of the CAP on the relative pricing of other products also impacts on fruit and vegetable consumption and needs to be examined (see page 43).

Monitoring by the European Union will be important. The Court of Auditors could assess the situation once the reformed regime has been in operation for two years, for example, and follow up its 1989 report.

6   **The European Union should, under Article 129 on public health of the Maastricht Treaty, ensure that its policies support the promotion of vegetables and fruit across Europe.**

Historically, nutrition has not been given much consideration in European agricultural or other policies. The Maastricht Treaty has established a protocol for public health input into policy under Article 129 which states that "Health protection requirements shall form a constituent part of the Community's other policies."

Article 129 should be used to ensure that policies in Europe do not act against improving availability and access to fruit and vegetables. Organisations working in Europe will need to lobby to ensure that this happens.

The European Union is a potential source of funding for promoting fruit and vegetables. Large producer groups have been able to harness European Union funds to promote consumption of fruit and vegetables and other UK producers will need to act collectively to access available funding.

Government

7   **The government should take a strategic lead in promoting vegetable and fruit consumption, by making an explicit commitment to supporting a sustained multi-sectoral strategy.**

There is currently no properly articulated government policy on food and nutrition. However, national health strategies such as *The Health of the Nation*[5] and *Scotland's Health: A Challenge to Us All*[6] provide a framework for change and have shown that cross-government commitment at Cabinet level is possible. In order to take forward the work done under those strategies by the Nutrition Task Force and Scottish Diet Action Group, the government needs to demonstrate leadership, and commitment to the issue of increasing vegetable and fruit consumption at Cabinet level.

This is one area where what is good for health is also good for business, particularly for the UK growing industry. For this reason, the Ministry of Agriculture, Fisheries and Food (MAFF), the Department of Health (DoH) and their equivalents in Scotland, Wales and Northern Ireland should take the lead.

The government should demonstrate leadership by setting up a strategy to increase fruit and vegetable consumption. It could bring together the various players and fund initiatives to kick start a national information campaign. The government should also coordinate research needs. Practical guidance on effective interventions may be useful and the government could fund the production of national guidelines.

8   The government should examine its own policies and ensure that policies in all departments do not undermine the goal of increasing vegetable and fruit consumption.

The impact of policies from all relevant government departments on public health, including nutrition, need to be assessed, as described in *Policy Appraisal and Health*,[7] and taken into account. The government could consider other wide-ranging strategies as potential models of cross-government involvement. One such model may be the UK strategy for sustainable development.[8]

While MAFF and the Department of Health and their UK equivalents should take the lead, policies in all government departments should be assessed to ensure that they support the aim of increasing vegetable and fruit consumption. For example, the Department for Education and Employment should ensure that the school curriculum and school meal provision encourage vegetable and fruit consumption among school children. Similarly, the Department of the Environment should take into account access to affordable fruit and vegetables when developing town planning policies. For example, making food a focus of local economic regeneration is one way to apply existing political will for change to the fruit and vegetable issue.

Food industry

9   Food retailers, in particular supermarkets, should develop new and innovative ways of promoting vegetables and fruit and improve local access to vegetables and fruit.

Developing new and innovative ways of promoting vegetables and fruit
Food retailers, especially the major multiple retailers, are important in shaping consumer choice and demand for foods. The relationship between retailers and their suppliers (growers or food manufacturers) along with their high profile promotional campaigns, means that they can have huge influence on UK eating patterns. Supermarkets now account for 67% of the fresh vegetables sold in the UK.

Supermarkets have expert knowledge and experience of promotional techniques and many are already involved in attempts to promote vegetables and fruit. These efforts could be extended to encourage fruit and vegetable consumption and increase sales. Examples include distributing leaflets, providing cooking instructions for vegetables, organising in-store cookery demonstrations and recipe tastings, special pricing offers, displaying fruit at checkout points and promoting particular recipe ideas by placing recipe cards or leaflets near the key ingredients and positioning ingredients near to one another. Retailers could also make available electronic point of sale (EPOS) data for research on fruit and vegetable consumption.

Independent traders, including greengrocers, could use some of the promotion techniques above and could also modify consumer purchasing patterns through pricing, special promotions and imaginative shop displays.

Improving local access to vegetables and fruit

One of the basic problems with increasing vegetable and fruit consumption is that many people need better sources of good quality, affordable produce near their homes. There are now areas where it is very difficult for people to buy good quality fruit and vegetables at affordable prices. Journeys to stores with a bigger choice of fruit and vegetables at affordable prices can be financially or physically difficult for people living in these areas, which tend to be characterised by low car-ownership levels and high proportions of single-parent families and elderly people.

Currently, selling vegetables and fruit to people in these areas is a missed opportunity for the retailers. People on low incomes constitute almost one-third of UK households and therefore their total spending power is considerable.

Retailers should take these issues into account when deciding on store siting and look into other ways of improving local availability of and access to fruit and vegetables. Supermarkets could work with health promotion departments or community initiatives to explore ways of improving local access by assisting food co-operatives or organising mobile shopping facilities.

10 The remit of the Horticultural Development Council could be extended to cover promotional and educational activities. Industry support for this would be needed.

The growing industry is a fragmented group and traditionally has taken little action collectively. In 1993, only £2.9 million was spent on advertising fruit and vegetables compared to the £71 million budget on chocolate and confectionery advertising. The low public awareness of the benefits of vegetables and fruit is not surprising given this relatively small sum spent on promotion. The degree of support for change varies between the different sectors of the fruit and vegetable growing industry; not surprisingly, some producers are wary of generic fruit and vegetable promotion in case it generates demand for overseas produce and increases imports.

There are examples of effective collective action in other spheres. The Meat and Livestock Commission, for example, spent £10 million on generic advertising for meat in 1994-95. There has also been some recent activity within the growing sector to promote fruit and vegetables in the form of the *Get Fresh* campaign and the Fresh Fruit and Vegetable Information Bureau *Go for Five a Day* campaign.

The UK growing industry could benefit from taking more action on a collective basis through, for example, the Horticultural Development Council (HDC). The HDC currently funds research and development for the UK growing industry, raising funds for this through its statutory levying powers. This remit of the HDC could be extended to include promotion and education so that more can be done collectively to promote fruit and vegetables. An increase in the HDC levy could cover this expanded remit. However, an attempt to raise the levy on growers is more likely to succeed if the government also offers financial support (see Chapter 5).

11 Growers need to be able to respond to changes in consumer demand. Growing patterns should be reviewed and new ways of improving links with consumers explored.

An increase in fruit and vegetable consumption is a great opportunity for British growers. To grasp this opportunity, however, the growing industry should gear itself up to respond to an increase in demand. UK growers need to review the types of fruit and vegetables they are growing, and the way they are presented, and explore opportunities for extending the range of produce, to match current and future trends in fruit and vegetable consumption. Market forecasts, by the HDC or other producer organisations for example, could help growers become more responsive to consumers.

Local supply mechanisms also need to be enhanced. The supermarkets already recognise the economic sense of using local producers to some extent, and some retailers have collaborated with regional initiatives to promote local produce. Retailers and growers should work together to encourage local supply. Improving such links could also help meet environmental concerns about the distances food products travel from producer to consumer.

Links between growers and consumers could also be improved through, for example, farmers' markets, farm shops and box schemes, where produce is delivered direct to consumers. Growers could also collaborate with community initiatives and might explore ways of distributing surplus produce to schools or nurseries (see Recommendation 5).

12 Caterers should place more emphasis on the use and promotion of vegetables and fruit and dishes containing them. This includes caterers in commercial settings, the NHS, the workplace and in schools.

In 1994, people in the UK ate an average of almost three meals each week outside the home.[9] Thus, caterers have a tremendous opportunity to influence fruit and vegetable consumption patterns. Caterers can, for example, incorporate vegetables or fruit as ingredients in familiar foods, promote unusual fruit and vegetables or ways of serving them, or introduce price incentives to encourage fruit and vegetable consumption. Another tactic could be making sure that vegetables or a side salad are included in the price of meals.

Existing initiatives to promote healthy eating, such as the HeartBeat Award scheme, could be used to draw additional attention to vegetables and fruit. Contracts for catering should specify the amount of fruit and vegetable provision at every meal.

Health authorities and health professionals

13 NHS purchasers, provider units and health professionals should take a lead in establishing local alliances to increase vegetable and fruit consumption.

Health authorities should work closely with local authorities in establishing local alliances. These local alliances could include the local food industry, local employers, local schools and community food initiatives. The NHS has an important part to play in increasing fruit and vegetable consumption as it has a triple role to educate, advocate and act as example. As educator, health professionals should provide information about the health benefits of fruit and vegetables. As advocate, health authorities, boards or trusts could convene local steering groups to bring about the changes needed to improve access to and availability of fruit and vegetables locally. As an example, NHS purchasers and providers should be aware of their own influence and promote vegetable and fruit consumption on NHS premises.

Directors of Public Health could use their annual reports to review the availability of and access to vegetables and fruit. Health promotion departments could work with local food retailers on promotional strategies, and conduct local audits of facilities and activities to ensure that fruit and vegetables are readily accessible and promoted. Community dietitians and health promotion departments could also work with, or offer training to, caterers to encourage them to include vegetables and fruit in catering. Another important role for health authorities is in the evaluation of initiatives to increase fruit and vegetable consumption and research into what makes interventions successful.

14 Health professionals, in particular the primary care team and public health professionals, should promote the health benefits of fruit and vegetables and the 'at least five a day' message.

The primary care team members are the key interface between the NHS and its users and they tend to be perceived as trustworthy sources of information. It is essential, therefore, that GPs, nurses, health visitors, midwives and other health professionals promote the fruit and vegetables message when giving nutritional advice, taking into account what stage people are at in the 'stages of change' model (see Chapters 7 and 8). Dietitians and health promotion departments should support the primary care team in this area.

Professional training in nutrition – at basic, post-basic and in-service levels – is essential if this approach is to succeed. The bodies responsible for training health professionals should ensure that the nutrition education for professional training includes information on the health benefits of vegetable and fruit consumption. This might include short courses or briefing sessions. Members of the primary care team may also need training in communicating messages to the public, and in health promotion and behaviour change techniques.

Local authorities

15 Local authorities should take a lead in local alliances to promote fruit and vegetable consumption. This role should include retail and market planning, encouraging local supply schemes, funding community initiatives and helping evaluate interventions.

The potential influence of local authorities in promoting fruit and vegetables is tremendous. A key function of local authorities is their role in planning. Authorities have the power to encourage fresh produce markets and street markets, decide on the siting of supermarkets and, ultimately, improve access to vegetables and fruit for many. Planning guidelines should ensure that there is access to produce.

Local authorities could work closely with health authorities in establishing local alliances. These alliances could involve the food industry, local employers, schools and community initiatives. The work of these local alliances in supporting a national information campaign is crucial.

Local authorities should also support community-based initiatives. These could include food co-operatives, allotment schemes or box schemes (where producers deliver an assortment of seasonal vegetables and fruits directly to consumers), community cafés which promote fruit and vegetables, and food coupon schemes which offer discounts on fruit and vegetables. Sustained funding and a secure future would increase the chances of success with this type of initiative.

Local authorities should also ensure that catering contracts for schools and local authority premises encourage fruit and vegetable consumption (see Recommendation 16).

Schools

16 Schools should introduce school food policies which help children to build fruit and vegetables into the structure of the school day.

Children must be a focus of any strategy to increase the consumption of fruit and vegetables (see Recommendation 3). Current levels of vegetable and fruit consumption in children give cause for concern. Research has shown that early consumption patterns are carried through into adult life. School food policies should promote the 'at least five a day' goal, both through classroom teaching and the hidden curriculum of school meals, tuckshops and vending machines.

Contracts for school meals should specify how fruit and vegetables are included in school meal provision and should be monitored. A survey of 1,200 school children and school meals in Glasgow found that only 22% of children selected fruit and 23% selected vegetables at their school meal.[10] Catering specifications may state, for example, that a choice of two vegetables, a salad, fruit and fruit juice must be available at each meal and that fruit and vegetables must be used in dishes. School meal providers could ensure that meals provide at least two portions of fruit and vegetables.

Schools could consider novel and imaginative techniques to promote fruit and vegetables. Options include breakfast clubs, 'fruit-only breaks', healthy tuckshop initiatives, a mobile fruit van, school horticulture projects, healthy eating vending machines, taste tests to introduce pupils to new fruit and vegetables, Smart Cards or other schemes which reward fruit and vegetable choices. Education authorities, schools and nurseries could collaborate with local growers or retailers to explore provision of free or subsidised fruit.

Nutrition education for professionals working in schools and nurseries is important. The relevant training bodies should build on the work of the Nutrition Task Force and recommendations of the Scottish Diet Action Group to ensure that this takes place.

17 Schools and education authorities should ensure that children learn cooking skills, including how to prepare and cook vegetables and fruit.

One of the barriers to increasing vegetable and fruit consumption is the perception that they are boring, difficult to prepare and that there are limited ways of serving them. A lack of knowledge about vegetables and fruit – and what to do with them – is associated with a gradual loss of cooking skills in recent decades. This is partly due to changes in food manufacture and retailing and partly due to the changes in lifestyle patterns which mean that convenience is increasingly important.

In addition, the food element of school curricula has been reduced in recent years. Pupils now have very little practical experience of preparing and cooking food. Both the Nutrition Task Force in England and the Scottish Diet Action Group have called for a strengthening of the food element of the school curriculum and the reintroduction of practical experience. Across the UK, government education departments, the curriculum advisory bodies, education authorities and school governing bodies should act on these recommendations to firmly re-establish the teaching of food skills in schools.

Media

18 A coordinated and sustained national media campaign is needed to increase the positive image of vegetables and fruit. In particular, advertising agencies need to develop new and creative means to enhance the image of vegetables and fruit.

Media activity to promote fruit and vegetables has been organised by individual trade bodies and other organisations. There remains a need for a coordinated and sustained national media campaign which could pool resources to maximum effect.

Media experts stress that it is easier to promote a positive message rather than a negative one. This gives the 'at least five a day' message an advantage over much other nutrition advice (see Recommendations 1 and 2).

Tried and tested media techniques – used in advertising other products, in TV cookery programmes, and in women's magazines – could be harnessed to promote fruit and vegetables. Media professionals warn, however, that messages should not be promoted as 'worthy' and that concentrating on the health benefits of vegetables and fruit may be a turn-off for many consumers: the emphasis should instead be on improving the image of fruit and vegetables by portraying them as tasty, fun, interesting, convenient and easy to prepare. However, this conflicts with US research, which shows that those who were aware of the *5 A Day – for Better Health* message were more likely to eat more fruit and vegetables. It is important to raise awareness of the specific health benefits but it should be possible for campaigns to combine this approach with enhancing the image of vegetables and fruit in general.

It is also important that regulations and guidelines on nutrition and health claims do not prevent promotion of the health benefits of vegetables and fruit. Reliable criteria need to be established to ensure that claims are credible and that the public can have confidence in them.

Voluntary sector/consumer groups

19 Health charities and consumer groups should work with the food industry to promote fruit and vegetables.

Health charities and consumer groups have a vitally important role to play in any strategy to increase fruit and vegetable consumption. Charities often have much public support and, as they are seen as independent, their messages are credible. By promoting 'at least five a day' as a consistent message, the heart disease and cancer charities could have a major impact on professionals as well as the public. Consumer groups – another credible source – should also be involved in promoting the 'at least five a day' message and practical advice on how to reach the goal.

In addition, health and consumer groups could collaborate with industry – growers, manufacturers, retailers and caterers – to promote vegetables and fruit in innovative ways, possibly linking this with fundraising. They could, for example, produce information packs about the benefits of fruit and vegetables, jointly organise in-store promotions and demonstrations and set up behaviour change interventions.

Researchers and academics

20 Researchers should take a lead in assessing practical interventions to increase fruit and vegetable consumption. Funding agencies – such as government, industry and health charities – should encourage such research.

Research from other countries shows that interventions can work. Equally, smaller scale interventions in the UK have shown that progress can be made towards the 'at least five a day' goal. However, there remains a need for more evaluation of interventions to assess their overall impact. Research is needed at a national and a local level – from assessing the effects of a change in the school curriculum across the country to evaluating the impact of a local practical intervention.

Interventions need to be easy to repeat in different circumstances, cost-effective and sustainable. Evaluation should highlight factors linked to successful interventions and those which distinguish less successful initiatives. Information about the evaluation of interventions should be widely disseminated so that lessons can be learned.

A comprehensive review of interventions to increase vegetable and fruit consumption is needed to create a solid research base to complement the ongoing evaluation of projects. The food industry should make its research results available to feed into this review. Advertisers and the media could also make available their findings, such as audience research data. Funding agencies, such as government, health charities, consumer groups and the food industry, could encourage such a review to be undertaken.

There is also a need to estimate quantitatively the health benefits of increased vegetable and fruit consumption.

References

1   National Heart Forum. 1997. *Preventing Coronary Heart Disease: The Role of Antioxidants, Vegetables and Fruit.* London: The Stationery Office.

2   World Health Organization. 1990. *Diet, Nutrition and the Prevention of Chronic Diseases.* Technical Report Series: 797. Geneva: World Health Organization.

3   Department of Health. 1994. *Nutritional Aspects of Cardiovascular Disease. Report of the Cardiovascular Review Group, Committee on Medical Aspects of Food Policy. Report on Health and Social Subjects 46.* London: HMSO.

4   The Scottish Office. 1993. *The Scottish Diet. Report of a Working Party to the Chief Medical Officer for Scotland.* Edinburgh: The Scottish Office Home and Health Department/HMSO Scotland.

5   Department of Health. 1992. *The Health of the Nation: A Strategy for Health in England.* London: HMSO.

6   The Scottish Office. 1992. *Scotland's Health: A Challenge to Us All:* Edinburgh: HMSO.

7   Department of Health. 1995. *Policy Appraisal and Health.* London: HMSO.

8   Department of the Environment. 1994. *Sustainable Development: the UK Strategy. Command Paper 2426.* London: HMSO.

9   Ministry of Agriculture, Fisheries and Food. 1995. *National Food Survey 1994.* London: HMSO.

10   Armstrong J. 1996. *A survey of the energy and nutrient composition and choice of fruit and vegetables in school meals selected by a sample of schoolchildren in Strathclyde.* Thesis for a Master of Public Health. Glasgow: University of Glasgow.

While the recommendations set out in this Chapter had considerable support from the large majority of participants, they do not necessarily reflect the views of all individuals at the expert meeting.

Part 2

Vegetables and fruit: the gap between recommendations and current consumption

Chapter 1

Recommendations and current consumption patterns: how big is the gap?

Carol Williams

Nutrition consultant

Introduction

Dietary and health advice encouraging the public to eat fruit and vegetables is not new. Nutrition education initiatives have always placed fruit and vegetables in a separate 'food group' and promoted them as a source of vitamins or 'protective factors'. The general advice to the public to eat plenty of fruit and vegetables has been consistent, even if its basis has changed as public health concerns have shifted from prevention of deficiency diseases to prevention of chronic health problems.[1] The current interest in vegetables and fruit stems largely from the evidence of the benefits of diets rich in antioxidants. (For more information see the National Heart Forum report *Preventing Coronary Heart Disease: The Role of Antioxidants, Vegetables and Fruit.*[2])

Until recently, health education messages about fruit and vegetables have simply advised consumers to eat 'more'. This gave no indication of how much was reasonable, and allowed complacency about present levels of consumption. A study in Scotland found that, among respondents with low intakes of vegetables and fruit (fewer than two portions a day), 55% thought that they were eating enough and already eating 'more'.[3] More recently, quantified national targets and individual advice have been introduced.

Recommended levels

In the United States, quantified advice was introduced in 1989, with a recommendation to eat 'five or more servings of a combination of vegetables and fruit daily'.[4]

The first quantified advice on fruit and vegetables in the UK followed publication of the World Health Organization's report on chronic disease prevention.[5] Based on apparently healthy fruit and vegetable intakes of populations living in southern Mediterranean countries with low rates of coronary heart disease, the World Health Organization (WHO) proposed a lower population limit of 400g of fruit and vegetables per person per day. The non-governmental organisations responsible for launching the WHO report in the UK translated this population goal into individual advice to 'eat at least five portions of fruit and vegetables a day' based on five 'decent sized' portions of about 80g[6, 7] (see page 22). Subsequently, advice to 'eat at least five' has been used in the popular media, leaflets and promotions produced by most of the major retailers in the UK and in a campaign by the Europe Against Cancer programme.[8]

The first quantified recommendation on fruit and vegetables from official sources in the UK came from *The Scottish Diet* report published in 1993.[9] It recommended that the Scottish public should double their intake of fruit and vegetables so that the average population intake in Scotland would be at least 400g per day. At the end of 1994, the COMA report on *Nutritional Aspects of Cardiovascular Disease*[10] recommended a 50% increase in fruit and vegetable consumption, which would mean a total recommended intake of approximately six portions of vegetables or fruit per person per day.

Identifying the gap between recommendations and current consumption

Identifying the gap between health recommendations on fruit and vegetables and current levels of consumption is not easy. The sources of data available at a national level are limited (see page 24) and the recommendations themselves are somewhat ambiguous. For example, what is meant by 'fruit and vegetables'? Does it include potatoes, fruit juice and products such as fruit yogurt or tomato soup? (See Table 1.) What amount of food constitutes a 'portion'? Definitions for these issues are proposed below. Less certain is whether recommendations to 'double' or 'increase by 50%' refer to the average intake of fruit and vegetables of the population as a whole, to subgroups of the population, or to individuals. The implications of these differences are discussed on page 32.

Which foods should be included in 'vegetables and fruit'?

There is no universally accepted convention on which foods should be included in health advice on fruit and vegetables, as Domel et al note in their aptly titled paper *"To be or not to be . . ." Fruits and vegetables.*[11] This is more than an academic concern to re-categorise what gardeners, greengrocers and retailers would take to be common sense. Health advice to eat more fruit and vegetables is based on their broad range of health and nutritional properties, their value as a source of dietary fibre and antioxidants, and as low fat, relatively low energy dense foods which can displace other less nutritious (fatty and sugary) foods from the diet. Any working definition of 'fruit and vegetables' needs to reflect these properties and take account of the social and cultural uses of different types of foods and the role of fruit and vegetables in constructing a balanced diet.

Table 1 *Controversial foods and advice on fruit and vegetables*

Conclusion	Rationale
Exclude potatoes. Exclude other starchy staples such as yams, cassava and plantain when eaten as a starchy staple. Include root crops such as carrots, swedes and turnips eaten in addition to main starchy staple.	Biologically, potatoes are a vegetable, but dietetically they are a 'starchy staple' (a major source of complex carbohydrate). They are used in place of other starchy staples and main carbohydrate sources such as bread, pasta or rice. They are not used interchangeably with other vegetables. This is in keeping with the *Balance of Good Health* food selection guide for the UK.[13]
Include fruit juice. Fruit juice should only 'count' once towards the 'at least five a day' recommendation, so that consumers do not think they can achieve 'five' by simply drinking fruit juice.	Fruit juice can provide most of the vitamins and minerals of fresh fruit, but the structure of the food is disrupted and most of the fibre is lost. Most of the intrinsic fruit sugars in the fruit will have become extrinsic sugars during juice extraction, and more cariogenic.
Exclude fruit drinks, squashes and cordials.	Most fruit drinks, squashes and cordials do not contain sufficient fruit juice.
Include frozen and canned fruit and vegetables.	Frozen fruit and vegetables have similar, and sometimes better, nutritional profiles than fresh fruit and vegetables. Consumers should be encouraged to choose produce tinned without sugar or salt.
Include baked beans and other pulses.	Pulses are rich in fibre, virtually fat-free and a useful source of iron and protein. However, they do not provide significant amounts of the antioxidant vitamins A, C or E. Dietary advice is that pulses are an alternative to meat, but also 'count' towards fruit and vegetables. Baked beans are one of the few vegetables eaten by many people who consume low amounts of fruit and vegetables, particularly children. Encouraging people to eat 'at least five' is less off-putting when they start from a base of one or two portions currently consumed, rather than zero.
Exclude nuts.	Nuts are usually consumed in small quantities as a snack item and contribute little to the average UK diet.
Include dried fruit. Use portions based on the equivalent wet weight. Supporting advice needs to stress the importance of variety and getting the rest of the five portions from other fruit and vegetables.	Although dried fruit is a source of dietary fibre and various vitamins and minerals, the drying process converts much of the intrinsic fruit sugar to extrinsic and destroys most labile vitamins such as vitamin C. Dried fruit is also highly energy dense, and including dried fruit in 'fruit and vegetables' could encourage consumption of dried fruit outside a meal. However, dried fruit clearly is a fruit.
Include composite (recipe) or processed foods provided they contain sufficient amounts of fruit and vegetable ingredient.	The fruit in a fruit pie, or the vegetables in a ready meal, can contribute towards the 'at least five' advice, irrespective of the fat or sugar content of the other ingredients. To 'count' as one portion, the fruit or vegetable needs to be present in sufficient quantity. For example, if the amount of apple in a serving of apple pie is equivalent to a whole apple, it 'counts' as one portion.
Some processed foods are unlikely to contain sufficient fruit or vegetable ingredient and are excluded: for example ketchup, processed vegetable soups, fruit cakes and yogurts.	Some processed foods, for example, fruit jam and fruit drinks, retain relatively little of the nutritional quality of the ingredient. Others contain very small amounts of fruit or vegetables.

Source: See reference 12.

The government's Nutrition Task Force, in England, set up a subgroup to advise on practical messages on the consumption of certain foods including fruit and vegetables[12] (see Chapter 4). It concluded that 'fruit and vegetables' includes fruit juice, baked beans and other pulses, dried fruit, and fruit and vegetables which are frozen, canned or used as main ingredients in recipes or composite foods, and excludes potatoes and nuts. The rationale for these conclusions is summarised in Table 1. This definition of fruit and vegetables has been used throughout this Chapter.

People will no doubt continue to debate the relative merits of including or excluding certain of the more contentious fruit and vegetable items within the proposed definition. For example, some organisations advocate fresh produce and question why frozen, canned and processed fruit and vegetables are included in the definition, despite evidence that frozen vegetables often contain higher levels of vitamin C than fresh. However, some kind of working definition and pragmatic agreement between health professionals about what is meant by fruit and vegetables is essential so that consumers can be provided with health information which is clear and practical.

The exclusion of potatoes is an issue which prompts much discussion but health advice consistently makes separate recommendations for starchy foods such as potatoes. COMA recommended a 50% increase in "bread, potatoes, and fruit and vegetables". Potatoes are not generally used in the same way as other vegetables. Most people would not consider having pasta with sauce and potatoes. It is worth noting that although potatoes are included in the *5 A Day* programme in the United States (see Chapter 8), crisps and chips (French fries) are excluded. A key difference is the high consumption of sweet potatoes and yams which differentiates US consumption patterns from those in the UK. Definitions of fruit and vegetables need to reflect the consumption patterns of the populations they apply to.

How much is a 'portion'?

A distinction can be made between a 'portion' and a 'serving'. A portion is a pre-defined amount of food. A serving is the amount an individual serves himself or herself, or is served, and is variable. There are no data available on how many portions/servings must be eaten in the typical UK diet to achieve a population target of 400g per person per day. Nor are there any accurate figures available on the number of servings/portions of fruit or vegetables currently consumed. Existing surveys record either total intake (the weight of fruit and vegetables eaten), or the frequency of consumption (the number of times each day).

However, the Ministry of Agriculture, Fisheries and Food[14] publishes average serving sizes recorded in dietary studies where individuals weigh the amounts of food they eat. By comparing these average serving sizes with the total weights of foods consumed, it is possible to estimate the number of portions eaten. This calculation suggests that nutrition information to 'eat five', which assumes a mean portion size of around 80g, ties in well with average serving sizes used by households in Britain (see Table 2). Therefore, by and large, practical advice to consumers does not need to advocate larger servings or go into detail about how much counts as a portion, but simply needs to recommend eating average amounts.

An example of practical descriptions of typical servings or portions is given in Table 3. The main area of discrepancy is with salad where serving sizes are much smaller. Education messages on eating 'five portions' therefore need to explain that it is necessary to eat a bowlful of salad to count towards the target.

Table 2 *Examples of average serving sizes taken from weights recorded in recent dietary surveys*

Food	Average serving size
Medium apple (without core)	100g
Medium banana (without peel)	100g
Average serving of Brussels sprouts	90g
Medium serving of boiled carrots	80g
Average medium serving of peas	70g
Medium tomato	85g

Source: See reference 14.

Table 3 *Example of portion advice for consumers*

Food type	Practical description of portion (approx 80g)	Examples
Fruit		
Very large fruit	One large slice	Melon, pineapple
Large fruit	One whole	Apple, banana
Medium fruit	Two whole	Plum, kiwi
Berries	One cupful	Raspberries, grapes
Stewed and canned fruit	Three serving spoonfuls	Stewed apple, canned peaches
Dried fruit	Half serving spoonful	Apricots, raisins
Fruit juice	Full wine glass	Orange juice (fresh and from concentrate)
Vegetables		
Green vegetables	Two serving spoonfuls	Broccoli, spinach
Root vegetables	Two serving spoonfuls	Carrots, parsnips
Very small vegetables	Three serving spoonfuls	Peas, sweetcorn
Pulses and beans	Two serving spoonfuls	Baked beans, kidney beans
Salad	Bowlful	Lettuce, tomato

Notes

1   The term 'serving spoonful' has been used to stress that the amounts of fruit and vegetables are as served onto the plate, rather than raw ingredients.
2   Supporting advice should explain that serving size should reflect age, sex and activity. Children can also 'eat at least five', but portions may be smaller.

Current levels of consumption

The main source of regular, up-to-date information on dietary intakes in the UK is the annual National Food Survey. This is a household survey which measures purchases and supply (foods brought into the home), rather than actual amounts consumed. The figures for fruit and vegetables include the weights of peel, core and outside leaves which are not eaten. Using factors for the 'edible portion' from McCance and Widdowson,[15] actual intakes have been estimated to be around 20% lower.[1] The most recent data available to the COMA Committee were from the 1992 National Food Survey.[16] Adjusting these figures for 'edible portion', the average population intake of fruit and vegetables was about 250g per day. COMA's recommended 50% increase in consumption would therefore mean a population target of about 375g per day. Figures from the 1994 National Food Survey[17] (adjusted for edible portion) similarly estimate average consumption to be about 250g. Using these adjusted figures and an average serving size of about 80g, it is estimated that current

Figure 1   *Frequency of eating fruit, by sex, 1994*

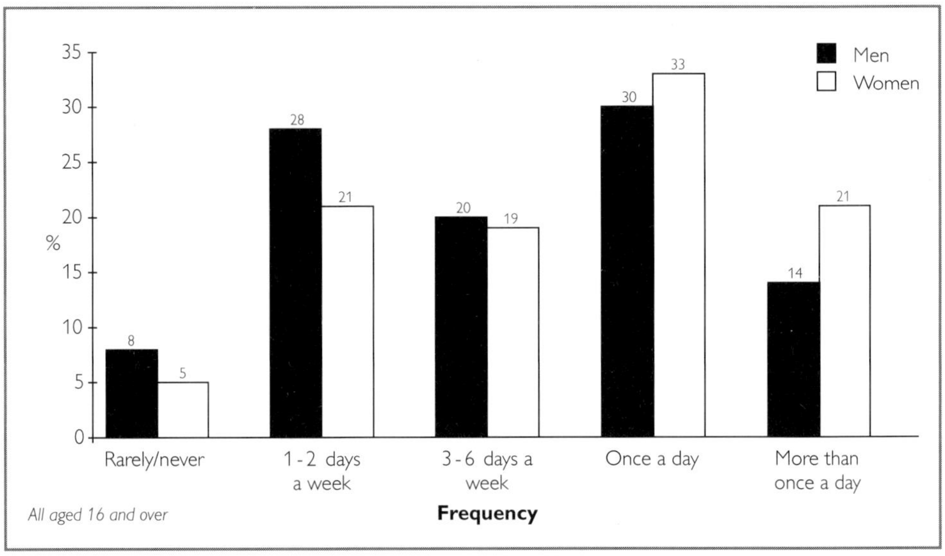

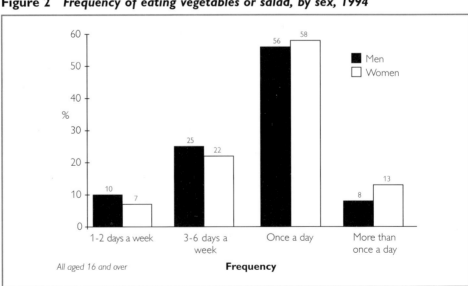

Source: See reference 18.

Figure 2   *Frequency of eating vegetables or salad, by sex, 1994*

Source: See reference 18.

At least five a day. Strategies to increase vegetable and fruit consumption

consumption is about three portions a day. This concurs with surveys of the frequency of fruit and vegetable consumption[18] which found that only 14% of men and 21% of women eat fruit more than once a day (see Figure 1), and 8% of men and 13% of women eat vegetables or salad more than once a day (see Figure 2).

The National Food Survey operates at the household level, so estimates of per capita consumption mask differences due to household composition. For example, young children could be expected to eat less. Furthermore, the survey gives no information about how the food brought into the home is divided between household members. Information about individual intakes is obtained by dietary intake studies which measure the weights of food consumed by the individual. The most recent national intake study of adults, *The Dietary and Nutritional Survey of British Adults*,[19] was carried out in 1986-1987. Figures from this survey similarly estimate average consumption of fruit and vegetables to be about 250g. No analysis of the number of servings consumed has been carried out.

These estimates of mean intakes of fruit and vegetables disguise variations by socioeconomic group, region, age and sex (see below).

Variations by socioeconomic group

The Dietary and Nutritional Survey of British Adults found a marked social gradient in intake of fruit and vegetables (see Table 4).[20] This is replicated in surveys looking at the frequency of consumption (see Figures 3 and 4), suggesting that strategies to increase consumption in lower socioeconomic groups need to focus on how often people eat fruit and vegetables, as well as how much is consumed.

Table 4 *Fruit and vegetable consumption in different socioeconomic groups*

g per person per day

Socioeconomic group	I & II		III Non-manual		III Manual		IV & V	
	Men	Women	Men	Women	Men	Women	Men	Women
Fruit	86g	98g	72g	100g	53g	61g	48g	50g
Vegetables	166g	142g	143g	132g	142g	113g	137g	106g
Fruit juice	57g	55g	40g	47g	28g	27g	12g	31g
Total fruit, vegetables and fruit juice per day	309g	295g	255g	279g	223g	201g	197g	187g
Total, men and women combined	302g		267g		212g		192g	

All aged 16-64
Mean consumption of fruit and vegetables = 244g per day

Source: See reference 20.

Figure 3 *Proportion eating fruit more than once a day, by sex and socioeconomic group, 1994*

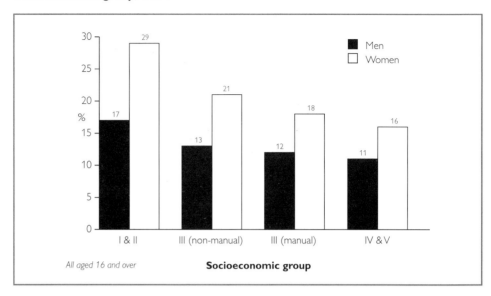

Source: See reference 18.

Figure 4 *Proportion eating vegetables or salad more than once a day, by sex and socioeconomic group, 1994*

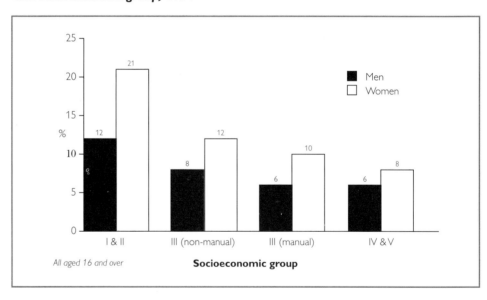

Source: See reference 18.

At least five a day. Strategies to increase vegetable and fruit consumption

Variation by region

Data from the National Food Survey suggest that there are regional variations in fruit and vegetable intakes, but this cannot be described as a clear north/south trend (see Figures 5 and 6). However, consumption is lower in Scotland, and it seems appropriate that *The Scottish Diet* report advocated a doubling of current consumption levels, that is a 100% increase, rather than COMA's recommended 50% increase.

Figure 5 *Household consumption of fruit, by region, 1994*

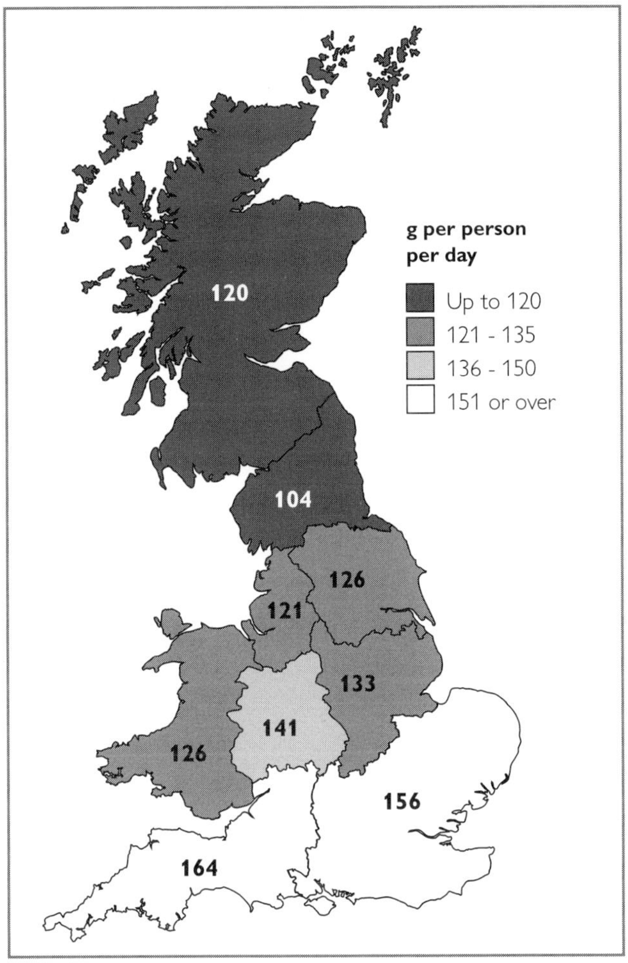

Source: See reference 21.

Figure 6   Household consumption of vegetables, by region, 1994

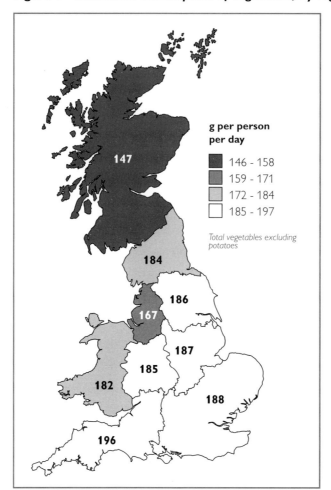

g per person
per day

■ 146 - 158
■ 159 - 171
□ 172 - 184
□ 185 - 197

Total vegetables excluding potatoes

Source: See reference 21.

It is unclear how much of the regional variation in fruit and vegetable consumption can be explained by differences in sociodemographic or socioeconomic factors. Researchers looking at intra-urban variation in reported food consumption in Glasgow[22] found that variations in the consumption of fruit and vegetables between four neighbourhoods in Glasgow persisted even after controlling for sex, age and social class. It was suggested that the cultural and supply factors need to be taken into account. If such differences can be detected within a single city, it seems reasonable to expect that cultural and supply differences between regions will have an effect nationally.

Variation by age

There appears to be a clear trend for older people to consume more fruit and vegetables than young people. This is evident from the National Food Survey data broken down by the age of the main diary-keeper, which show that younger households eat less fresh fruit and vegetables and slightly more processed vegetables (see Figure 7). Older people consume fruit and vegetables more frequently than the young. Among 16–24 year olds, 66% consume fruit less than once a day, and 48% consume vegetables and salad less than once a day.[23]

Figure 7 *Household consumption of fruit and vegetables by age of main diary-keeper, 1994*

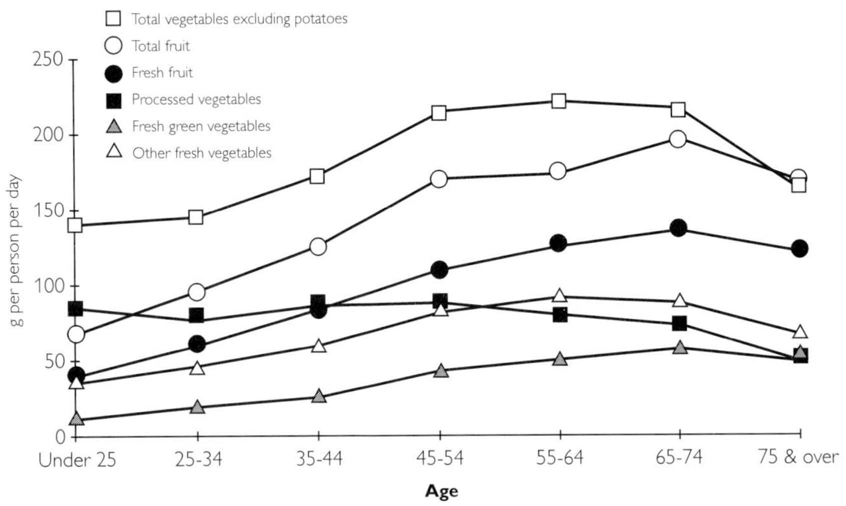

Other fresh vegetables excludes potatoes. Processed vegetables includes chips and crisps.

Source: See reference 21.

Trends in vegetable and fruit consumption

According to National Food Survey data there has been a gradual increase in the consumption of fruit and vegetables (excluding potatoes and potato products) since the late 1950s (after the end of rationing) from about 250g per person per day to about 300g[10] (see Figure 8). These figures, however, include the weights of peel, core and outsides leaves which are not eaten (see page 24). This increase has been mainly due to increases in frozen vegetables, salad vegetables, citrus fruits and fruit juices. Consumption of more traditional vegetables such as swedes, parsnips and Brussels sprouts has declined.

Figure 8 *Trends in consumption of vegetables and fruit*

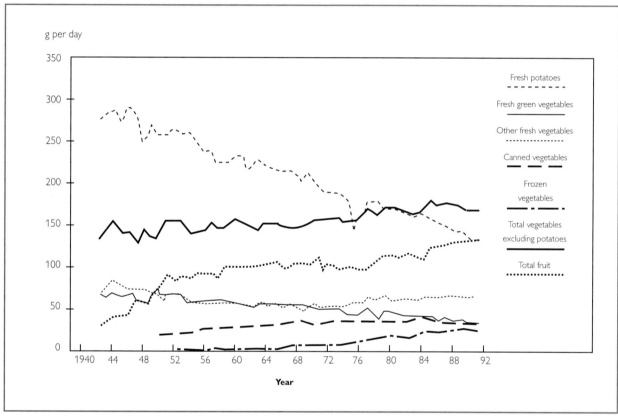

Source: See reference 10.

At least five a day. Strategies to increase vegetable and fruit consumption

Comparison with other European Countries

The United Nations Food and Agriculture Organization collects annual statistics of per capita national food supply (production plus imports less exports and non-food uses). Although these figures tend to over-estimate amounts actually consumed because they make no allowance for domestic waste, they are a useful source of comparative data. Compared with other countries in Europe, consumption in the UK is about half that of Greece, Italy and Spain (see Figure 9).

Figure 9 *Fruit and vegetable consumption in Europe, 1992*

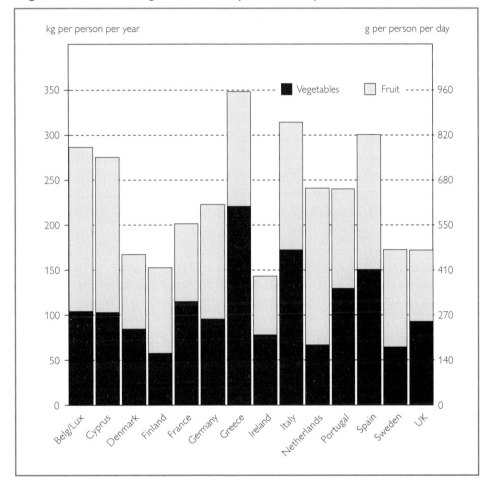

Source: See reference 24.

Reaching the recommendations

It is unclear from the recommendations whether national dietary targets of 400g (as recommended in Scotland) or a 50% increase (as recommended by COMA) are intended to be applied to different subgroups of the population. Achieving a mean intake of 400g would achieve a fairly modest 30% increase in consumption for people in higher socioeconomic groups, but a doubling or 100% increase for those in manual groups. Conversely, applying a relative target such as COMA's 50% increase would have the effect of widening the differences between subgroups: for example, a 50% increase in intakes in lower socioeconomic groups from 190g to 285g per day, compared to 450g in higher socioeconomic groups. Similarly, if advice for the public to double their consumption of fruit and vegetables (as recommended in Scotland) was applied to individuals, this would increase the difference between high and low consumers.

Health professionals making use of these targets need to keep in mind the need to ensure that the benefits of eating plenty of fruit and vegetables are conferred upon the population subgroups which need them most. This means applying absolute and relative targets at the population level with appropriate discretion, and making use of absolute targets such as 'at least five a day' at the individual level. There has been some criticism of this approach for having an over-emphasis on figures.* However, research has indicated that the public need a goal they can aim for.[25]

It is clear that, to achieve the health recommendations, people need to eat both vegetables and fruit more than once a day. Some health advice in the US has specified 'eat at least 3 servings of vegetables and 2 servings of fruit daily'.[26] The challenge is to find strategies which will achieve a regular increase so that fruit and vegetables are incorporated into a daily pattern. This means identifying opportunities for introducing more fruit and vegetables, for example, eating fruit at breakfast, or serving two vegetables with a meal. Three sample daily patterns are given in Table 5.

The COMA Committee noted that consumption of fruit and vegetables has risen since the 1940s, mainly due to increases in frozen vegetables, salad, citrus fruits and fruit juices.[10] However, consumption of more traditional vegetables such as swede, parsnips and sprouts has declined. This trend has implications for both the economic and the environmental impact of health advice to increase consumption of fruit and vegetables.[27] Increasing imports of fruits and vegetables will affect the balance of trade and incur a greater environmental cost due to the energy cost of transportation. Perhaps there is a need to think not so much of the Mediterranean diet, but of Mediterranean proportions, and to encourage consumption of domestically produced fruits and vegetables.

---

*   Population goals such as the World Health Organization's '400g a day' are intended for use by policy makers; it is not suggested that the weight of fruit and vegetables should be used in messages to the general public. Such figures are a benchmark against which to assess average levels of fruit and vegetable consumption in the population.

Table 5   Three ways to get 'at least five a day'

	Portions
The 'office worker'	
Morning	
Fruit juice	1
Breakfast cereal with sliced banana on top	1
Cup of tea	
Lunchtime	
Sandwich with lots of salad inside, plus tomato and celery stick	1
Apple	1
Evening	
Pasta with tomato-based sauce and broccoli	1½
Total	**5½ portions**
The 'slimmer'	
Morning	
Half a grapefruit	1
Cup of coffee	
Lunchtime	
Baked potato with vegetable filling such as ratatouille or baked beans	1
Mid-afternoon	
Peach	1
Evening	
Vegetable hot-pot	2
Total	**5 portions**
The 'traditional'	
Morning	
Fruit juice	1
Toast and marmalade	
Cup of tea	
Lunchtime	
Vegetable soup and bread roll	1
Piece of cake	
Cup of tea	
Evening	
Lamb chop, potatoes, carrots and sprouts	2
Rhubarb crumble and custard	1
Total	**5 portions**

References

1   Williams C, Marmot M. 1997. In: National Heart Forum. *Preventing Coronary Heart Disease: The Role of Antioxidants, Vegetables and Fruit.* Changing rationales, consistent advice: dietary recommendations on vegetables and fruit. London: The Stationery Office.

2   National Heart Forum. 1997. *Preventing Coronary Heart Disease: The Role of Antioxidants, Vegetables and Fruit.* London: The Stationery Office.

3   Anderson A, Marshall D, Lean MEJ, Foster A. 1994. Ripe for change: Fruit and vegetables in Scotland – Current patterns and potential for change. *Health Bulletin;* 52: 1: 51-64.

4   National Research Council. 1989. *Diet and Health: Implications for Reducing Chronic Disease Risk.* Food and Nutrition Board Committee on Diet and Health. Washington DC: National Academy Press.

5   World Health Organization. 1990. *Diet, Nutrition and the Prevention of Chronic Diseases.* Technical Report Series: 797. Geneva: World Health Organization.

6   Coronary Prevention Group and Guild of Food Writers. 1991. *Eat Well, Live Well.* London: Coronary Prevention Group.

7   Marshall J, Heughan A. 1992. *Eat for Life Diet.* London: Vermilion.

8   Cancer Education Coordinating Group, Europe Against Cancer. 1994. *A Key to Health: Eat Fruit and Vegetables Every Day.* London: Europe Against Cancer.

9   The Scottish Office. 1993. *The Scottish Diet. Report of a Working Party to the Chief Medical Officer for Scotland.* Edinburgh: The Scottish Office Home and Health Department/HMSO Scotland.

10   Department of Health. 1994. *Nutritional Aspects of Cardiovascular Disease. Report of the Cardiovascular Review Group, Committee on Medical Aspects of Food Policy. Report on Health and Social Subjects 46.* London: HMSO.

11   Domel SB, Leonard SB, Baranowski T, Baranowski J. 1993. "To be or not to be . . ." Fruits and vegetables. *Journal of Nutrition Education;* 25: 6: 352-358.

12   Williams C. 1995. Healthy eating: Clarifying advice about fruit and vegetables. *British Medical Journal;* 310: 1453–1455.

13   Health Education Authority. 1994. *The Balance of Good Health: Introducing the National Food Guide.* London: Health Education Authority.

14   Ministry of Agriculture, Fisheries and Food. 1993. *Food Portion Sizes.* Second edition. London: HMSO.

15   Paul AA, Southgate DT. Royal Society of Chemistry and Ministry of Agriculture, Fisheries and Food. 1993. *McCance and Widdowson's The Composition of Foods.* Fifth edition. London: HMSO.

16   Ministry of Agriculture, Fisheries and Food. 1993. *Household Food Consumption and Expenditure 1992.* London: HMSO.

17   Ministry of Agriculture, Fisheries and Food. 1995. *Household Food Consumption and Expenditure 1994.* London: HMSO.

18   Office of Population Censuses and Surveys, Social Survey Division. 1996. *Health Survey for England 1994.* London: HMSO.

19   Gregory J, Foster K, Tyler H, Wiseman M for the Office of Population Censuses and Surveys. 1990. *The Dietary and Nutritional Survey of British Adults.* London: HMSO.

20   Ministry of Agriculture, Fisheries and Food. 1994. *The Dietary and Nutritional Survey of British Adults – Further Analysis.* London: HMSO.

21   Ministry of Agriculture, Fisheries and Food. 1995. *National Food Survey 1994.* London: HMSO.

22   Forsyth A, Macintyre S, Anderson A. 1994. Diets for Disease? Intraurban variation in reported food consumption in Glasgow. *Appetite;* 22: 3: 259–274.

23   Bennett N, Dodd T, Flatley J, Freeth S, Bolling K for the Office of Population Censuses and Surveys. 1995. *Health Survey for England 1993.* London: HMSO.

24   Food and Agriculture Organization Agrostat Supply Data.

25   Cox DN, Anderson AS, McKellar S, Reynolds J, Lean MEJ, Mela DJ. In press. Consumer strategies for increasing fruit and vegetable consumption in the UK. *Proceedings of the Nutrition Society.*

26   US Department of Health and Human Services. 1990. *Nutrition and Your Health: Dietary Guidelines for Americans.* Third edition. Home and Garden Bulletin No. 232. Washington DC: US Department of Agriculture and US Department of Health and Human Services.

27   Gussow JD. 1995. Mediterranean diets: are they environmentally responsible? *American Journal of Clinical Nutrition;* 61 (6 suppl): 1383S–1389S.

Chapter 2

Reaching the recommendations: what are the barriers?

Suzi Leather

Food policy consultant

Introduction

Not enough is known about the barriers to increased vegetable and fruit consumption. Most research is focused on individuals, rather than on caterers or retailers. This may be a legacy of 19th century individualism. Social problems tend to be seen in terms of individual psychological dispositions and personal inadequacies. This has been true of many studies of dietary choice. Rarely is there a systematic effort to characterise problems such as inadequate diet as a public ill.

Equally rare is the attempt to put present problems in an historical perspective. The particular problems of Britain's low vegetable and fruit consumption may lie with the country's early industrial revolution. People moved off the land much earlier than many European societies. Losing contact with the land may have cast a long shadow over the nation's dietary choices.

Whether or not a low consumption of vegetables and fruit is inextricably linked to modernism, all present-day barriers must be tackled – not only those amenable to individual solutions. This is especially so since many of the barriers lie in the public domain: in Britain's currently accepted role of the state, in its definitions of freedom, and in its political and social economy.

Barriers exist at various stages throughout the food chain, from production through to retailing and catering. The underlying problem is the willingness to tackle them. In school catering for instance, price margins, least-cost tendering and the problem of wastage are likely to be immediate barriers to increased vegetable and fruit consumption. But the underlying barrier is under-resourcing of education.

Links with the food culture and the food economy

The barriers to vegetable and fruit consumption are not random phenomena. They are embedded in social and economic structures: relationships, attitudes, and beliefs which govern our food culture. They exist in, and will change over time. Attitudes to what count as barriers will also change over time. How long will it be before aggressively promoted and marketed functional foods and dietary supplements are themselves seen as barriers to increasing vegetable and fruit consumption?

Since these barriers are social phenomena, they will themselves be subject to social change. Some trends mutually compound the problems: the population is ageing, and becoming less mobile and more frail, just at the time when local food shops are closing and consumers are forced to travel further to shop. A survey by Mintel predicted that by the year 2000, 30% of the population of the United Kingdom will form one-person households.[1] These consumers, especially the elderly people among them, need to be able to buy vegetables and fruit in small amounts. Pre-packing can be a barrier for many single householders.

Barriers also vary from person to person. For some the overriding problem is access – availability and price. People who have only £10 a week to spend on food will not buy many vegetables or fruits. How much money people have to spend on food depends on the other calls on their income. This can change quite rapidly: poorer consumers in the South West now spend 10% of their income on water.[2] An obvious barrier is that food money is not ring-fenced in any way. In fact the opposite is usually the case; food money is the area of expenditure offering the most flexibility.

If the price of vegetables and fruit has risen less than the price of meat or cereals for example, it does not follow that price is not a barrier.[3] People's purchasing priorities are a more significant factor. The important question is whether vegetables and fruit are regarded as a staple (a buy first) or as an extra (a bolt-on).

Changing food patterns

Changing food patterns also erect new barriers. Fruit has to compete with the hugely popular and relatively new potato products and dairy products. There is constant innovation in these branded goods. Fruit and vegetables may seem boring by comparison.

The changes in our preferred meal patterns mean that the 'slot' for vegetables is being gradually eroded. Vegetables were what we ate with our traditional sit-down main meal. They may not have constituted what we regarded as the main, or most important, part of it (people are still reluctant to regard a vegetable dish as a proper main meal), but the main meal was the vegetable slot. With the decline in popularity of the sit-down main meal, the vegetable slot also goes. Individualised solitary snacking is a barrier to increasing vegetable consumption. It is therefore necessary to construct alternative slots for fruit and vegetables, or create images of eating vegetables and fruit that fit in with our individualised lifestyles.

The shift towards convenience foods is also a barrier to increased vegetable and fruit consumption. For many people real food is what comes out of a tin or packet. Gone are the cooking skills which allowed people to cook and eat their own food from fresh ingredients. This not only makes people dependent on manufactured foods; it also changes people's attitudes towards 'ordinary' vegetables and fruit. The eclecticism of modern food culture does not seem to have extended beyond the 'main course' part. Chips are eaten with pizza, as readily as with burgers.

Even the one big shop a week routine is a barrier to increasing vegetable and fruit consumption because these foods spoil quickly. This is a particular problem for those who must avoid waste at all costs.

Political will

Not all the barriers are material barriers such as income, access, cooking skills, the problem of waste, and storage facilities. Other barriers are more abstract. They relate to the general political culture. The current 'hands off', minimalist role for government, ruling out intervention in what are seen as 'market' operations, is itself a barrier to increased vegetable and fruit consumption.

The way in which the national Nutrition Task Force in England[4, 5] has operated exemplifies this conception of proper government. It seems to have amounted to little more than acting as a kind of opportunity broker, bringing the parties together. There did not seem to be a willingness for government to throw its weight properly behind the initiatives of the various Nutrition Task Force project teams, or to identify and promote a collective interest. This highly limited role for government is a barrier to increased vegetable and fruit consumption, for it stymies attempts to build a coordinated base for marketing and promoting vegetables and fruit. And this is much needed.

A related barrier is the belief that there is no middle ground between the extremes of a command economy on the one hand and uncontrolled market forces on the other. Although there is no evidence that unrestricted market forces necessarily produce the best nutritional outcome, it has become very difficult to offer acceptable ways to structure or restrain food choices without the accusation that people's freedom is being interfered with.

This worry usually focuses on freedom as the absence of immediate constraints on choice. (Everyone is free to eat at the Ritz.) But the assumption that, if choice is left to the market, it will automatically be 'free' ignores the fact that powerful forces operate to constrain and mould those choices. Choices are not made in a vacuum but are shaped by commercial and economic constraints and by fashion. These are themselves social processes; there is nothing absolute or immutable about them.

A consequence of the hands-off role for government is that health education and food industry messages are allowed to co-exist with bewildering contradictions. Of course there are powerful forces opposed to anyone advocating healthy eating choices, and of course they make their views known to government. Manufacturers of foods which we need to eat less of (such as confectionery, cakes or biscuits) are bound to complain. This would not necessarily matter if there was a willingness either to limit, or at least match, the level of money spent on advertising these foods. But no such commitment exists. One of the reasons for this is that the UK does not have a properly articulated food and nutrition policy.

The lack of a food and nutrition policy is perhaps the ultimate barrier to increased vegetable and fruit consumption. The absence of a policy both signals the lack of importance accorded to nutrition, and denies a forum of sufficient stature where the implementation of policies which would overcome barriers to increased vegetable and fruit consumption could take place. There is not even a place where all the government departments with relevant interests meet and talk.

The report of the Low Income Project Team (LIPT) of the Nutrition Task Force[6] called for a national approach to food and low income. It did so because members recognised that overcoming many of the barriers to increased vegetable and fruit consumption involves identifying and restructuring the aspects of the food economy which result in low consumption of vegetables and fruit. A more radical consideration of the food and low income problem than LIPT was allowed would undoubtedly have looked at the need for price subsidies, distribution or transport subsidies, and increased welfare benefits. Certainly, the Nutrition Task Force began the debate; what is lacking is a clear direction for the Nutrition Task Force's work to continue in. This is itself a barrier to the increased consumption of vegetables and fruit.

'Structuring in' fruit and vegetable consumption

Political will meets individual will over the issue of whether we should 'structure in' fruit and vegetable consumption. When children automatically received a third of a pint of milk half way through the school morning, their calcium consumption was structured in. One of the barriers to increasing fruit and vegetable consumption is that there are so few structured opportunities for eating them. This could be changed; it would be possible to introduce school fruit. After all, the school curriculum allots time for exercise, so why not structure in a fruit slot?

Children's break times could become a crisp-, biscuit-, cake- and chips-free zone, with children only allowed to consume fruit or vegetables. Although many schools do operate such a policy, the suggestion that this be adopted nationally brings the most extraordinary opposition in the UK. And yet there are examples in other countries of schools which have no problems with a fruit-only policy.

In a study of children's attitudes towards fruit in Germany and England, Neale et al argue that the supply and promotion of fruit in schools needs to be improved.[7] Despite similar levels of knowledge and preferences, significant differences in consumption exist (see Figure 1).

Figure I *Which of the following do you bring for your school break?*

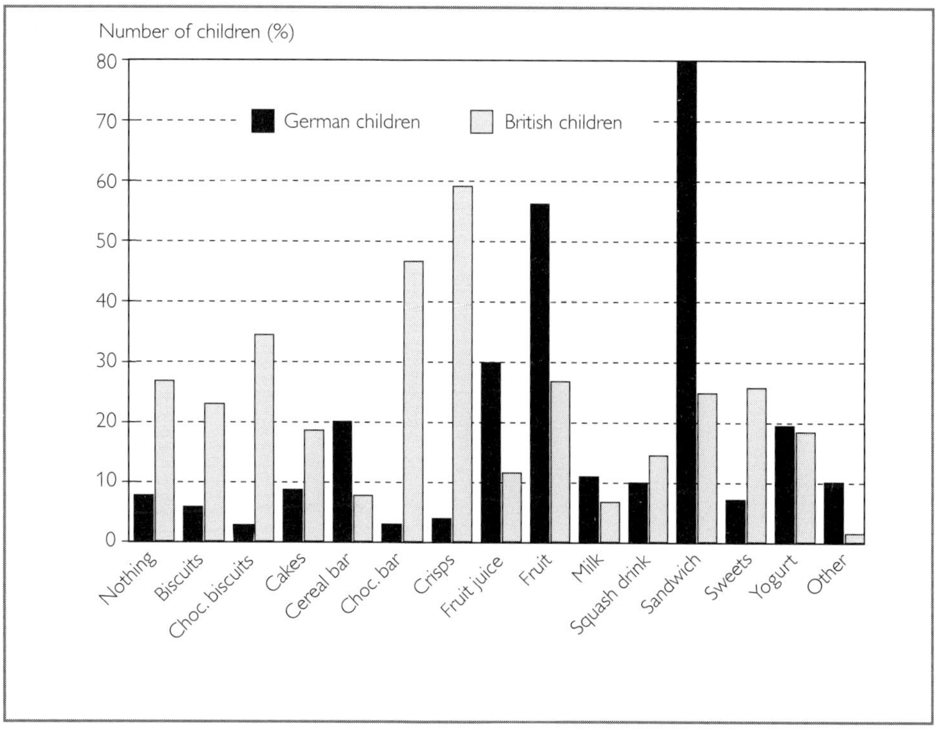

Source: See reference 7.

It would also be possible to help people increase their vegetable and fruit intake by structuring their buying habits. Research carried out by the Soil Association on box schemes (whereby producers deliver an assortment of seasonal vegetables and fruits directly to consumers on a regular basis), has shown that these direct marketing schemes help increase their customers' vegetable consumption.[8] Much more could be done to promote box schemes, widen their appeal and perhaps promote them in areas currently badly served by food retailers.

Barriers at the level of the individual

Income barriers: "I cannot afford it"

"Poverty attracts an unfortunate abundance of risks . . . the wealthy (in income, power, or education) can purchase safety and freedom from risk . . . the possibilities and abilities to deal with risks, avoid them or compensate for them are probably unequally divided among the various occupational or educational strata . . . a sufficiently well filled wallet puts one in a position to dine on eggs from 'contented hens' and salads from 'pampered heads of lettuce'. Education and attentiveness to information open up new possibilities of dealing with and avoiding risks."[9]

There is ample evidence that consumers living on low incomes, whether benefits or low wages, face significant problems in affording a healthy diet. They find it particularly difficult to manage to eat enough vegetables and fruit. Research identifying barriers to increasing vegetable and fruit consumption in the UK found that the cost of fruit was a barrier for 31% of consumers and the cost of vegetables a barrier to 23%.[10] Certainly families living on low incomes eat very much less vegetables and fruit than the better-off, and have correspondingly lower intakes of antioxidants. Consumption of vegetables and fruit is very sensitive to income, and the greatest nutritional inequalities are in antioxidants.[11]

Inadequate income also brings with it psychological and socialisation barriers. Food purchasing, particularly at the lower end of the market, becomes repetitive. Poorer consumers buy what they know they and their families like. There is little or no room for experimentation or, crucially for vegetables and fruit, for waste. This poses severe problems for increasing consumption of vegetables and fruit which are seen as risky products which go off and are wasteful.[12] It means that many people are missing a chance of being socialised into eating lots of vegetables and fruit. Inadequate income also affects the social choices we can make around food. Sharing a bag of crisps is like passing around a packet of cigarettes: it is a means of social connection. How can people be persuaded to see cutting up an apple into several pieces in the same light?

The weight barrier: "I can't carry them"
Some of the barriers, particularly those operating at the individual level, are mundane. However, it is important to remember these very ordinary, but nevertheless significant barriers. Elderly people probably find that the sheer weight of vegetables and fruit is a major disincentive to increasing their consumption. It is hard enough for them to carry home what they manage now. The weight problem is felt not only by elderly people; it is also a barrier for the 31% of the population who do not own a car,[13] those who shop by bus, and anyone who shops with a buggy and small children.

Food skills: "I don't know what to do with them"
There is room for improvement both of our knowledge of fruits and vegetables, and what to do with them. A social worker in Plymouth who specialises in deprivation problems explained why she thought some people did not eat more fresh vegetables and fruit: "It has lots to do with not having enough money. But it is also a matter of confidence and skill ... Basically loads of people don't know that you can use a potato peeler for other vegetables."[14]

"I do not want to change. I do not need to change"
When asked, we over-estimate our vegetable and fruit consumption and under-estimate our alcohol and cigarette consumption. These are probably rational ways to protect our self-esteem. Nevertheless, self-perceptions like these are also barriers to change and need to be explored if they are to be tackled effectively.

Most people think they have a good enough diet. They know the healthy eating messages, but do not think that the messages contained in them imply that they themselves need to change. *The Scottish Diet* report drew attention to misperception as a barrier to increased vegetable and fruit consumption.[15] Over 70% of Scots did not wish to change their current vegetable and fruit intake. Why?

Before jumping to any conclusions, these misperceptions need to be examined more closely. Do they not actually reveal deeper barriers which prevent people closing the gap between theory and practice? What is it that facilitates or prevents people from identifying with healthy eating messages? What are the issues involved with developing and maintaining an identity as a healthy person? Relevant issues may include:

- Where does the message about health behaviour come from? Is the source credible and trustworthy?

- Is the message put across in a way which people understand? What is 'a portion'?

- Do people feel capable of being, or even want to be, the kind of person who eats a lot of vegetables and fruit? Would eating more vegetables and fruit mean trading in a certain valued self-identity for an uncertain one? Do 'real men' eat fruit and vegetables?

- Do vegetables and fruit have enough social value?

- One of the barriers to increased fruit and vegetable consumption is precisely that the message is a health one. Many people are turned off by health messages.

- What are the pre-conditions for feelings of fatalism (there is nothing I can do to affect my future) versus feelings of autonomy or self-efficacy (I can affect my future)?

Replicating and mirroring the nutritional pyramid

Food consumption is the result of a complex interaction of forces as diverse as how foods are marketed and promoted, where they are sold and at what price, whether we know what to do with them, and the images they conjure up for us. The holy grail is for most people to achieve a pattern of food consumption in keeping with the nutritional pyramid, with the bulk of the diet being the daily staples – bread, cereals, rice, pasta, vegetables and fruit – and right at the top the foods that are rarely eaten, or only eaten in small amounts – sweets, eggs, red meat etc. That is the aim – the traditional healthy Mediterranean diet.

An obvious barrier is that we do not have the production, marketing, advertising and retailing structure to back it up. The Mediterranean diet is not just a particular mix of fruits and vegetables in a consumer's basket. It is as much the venue of the market itself, and the quality of the social and economic exchanges that take place there, as the fruits and vegetables which constitute it. It is also the amount of agricultural land devoted to those foods, the support given to growers, the cuisine which uses them; it is the entirety of the social and economic food substructure. The question for us is not as simple as whether consumers can buy a Mediterranean diet in the superstore food culture, but whether all these other aspects can be created.

Certainly it is not just a matter of changing individual consumer choice. Trying to increase our intake of vegetables and fruit is not as simple as buying three apples instead of two, or covering one-quarter of the plate with helpings of vegetables rather than one-sixth. Someone has got to grow the extra produce, or transport it across the world. And if people are eating all those extra vegetables and fruit, producers and manufacturers of other foods are going to miss out.

Increasing vegetable and fruit consumption necessitates reform in food retailing, in agricultural production methods, in the Common Agricultural Policy, and even in social security benefits scales. It requires agricultural production methods which mirror the nutritional pyramid, retail policies which mirror it, advertising campaigns which mirror it, and perhaps most controversially, pricing and income policies which mirror it.

Increasing fruit and vegetable consumption significantly would have knock-on effects on the economy not only on agricultural production but also on the balance of payments. The United Kingdom is only 88% self-sufficient in fresh vegetables, 19% self-sufficient in non-citrus fruit, and 0% self-sufficient in citrus fruit.[16]

If the UK population increased its intake of vegetables and fruit by 50% overnight, without any of the additional supply coming from an increase in domestic production, this would clearly have a devastating effect on the economy. The UK trade deficit in fruit and vegetables was already £2.8 billion in 1993.[17] There is a clear nutritional case for giving much more economic support to domestic growers, targeting that support according to nutritional criteria, and massively increasing the amount spent on advertising fruit and vegetables.

Promotion and marketing

As a sector, the fruit and vegetable producers are relatively weak in terms of collective clout, and fragmented in terms of organisation. Meat has the Meat and Livestock Commission, but there is really no comparative organisation for fruit and vegetables. This is an important barrier to increased consumption. It makes it difficult for the producer side of the fruit and vegetable food chain to act collectively. This in turn means that there is very little scope for generic advertising campaigns. In 1992 the Potato Marketing Board was the biggest fruit and vegetable advertising spender at £1.9 million, followed by Outspan with £1.5 million.[17] The Meat and Livestock Commission organises generic advertising and spent £10 million in 1994/95. These figures exclude the advertising of branded meat products by individual companies, which for that year amounted to £16.9 million.[18]

It is also worth examining how much is spent on advertising the foods which in many respects directly compete with fruit. In the UK in 1993, £2.9 million was spent advertising fresh fruits, vegetables and nuts. Nearly three times as much was spent advertising chewing gum, and £71.2 million was spent advertising chocolate confectionery.[19] Fruit and vegetables need to be promoted much harder. There should be substantial funding for the promotion of fruit and vegetables.

"You can't buy them round here"

The malign nutritional consequences of a deepening income inequality are all too obvious from the food consumption data, but the effects are felt not only by individual households. The national Low Income Project Team (LIPT) reported "There are whole communities with inadequate access to the constituents of a healthy diet. This is due in part to decisions on siting and stocking, and in part to the spatial concentration of poverty: when whole communities have very limited buying power this in turn limits the opportunities for retailers."[6]

The LIPT identified many of the barriers faced by deprived areas in getting access to healthy food. It set out a strategy for improving low income consumers' access to a healthy diet, including better access to affordable, good quality vegetables and fruit. The barriers to taking this strategy forward depend on two factors. Firstly whether local food projects, institutions of social solidarity, can get adequate and sustained funding. And secondly whether the food retail industry will see fit to work in partnership with local communities. Again the hands-off role of government will not advance the cause.

Common Agricultural Policy pricing

The destruction of fruit and vegetables under the Common Agricultural Policy (CAP) is an outrage, but in terms of barriers to increased fruit and vegetable consumption, the problems may in fact be more related to the price of foods other than fruit and vegetables. Some agricultural economists argue that the CAP in fact offers a price incentive to fruit and vegetable consumption since it does not increase the price of fruit and vegetables as much as some less healthy foods, such as animal fat and sugar. But perhaps this looks at the problem from the wrong end. The CAP is particularly harmful for low income consumers, not only because it puts up the price of food generally, and is a regressive tax, but because it significantly increases the price of those 'cheap' calories – fat and sugar – leaving less money for the bolt-ons – fruit and vegetables.

Conclusion

The barriers to reaching healthier consumption levels are entrenched in our food habits and beliefs. The material barriers are obvious and measurable. Harder to assess are the psychological or identity barriers. Food images are created commercially, largely through branded products. The nutritional needs, even of our children, are subordinated to the overriding requirement to keep costs down and allow food producers freedom at the expense of nutritional needs. Deprivation becomes a more, not less, pressing determinant of inadequate diet. There is no longer a sufficient will to support a social welfare network capable of meeting the basic needs of recipients.[20]

Many of these trends themselves are implicated in the wider patterns of what is coming to be called post-modernity – globalisation, marketisation, individualisation, the malleability of our identity. Some see these developments as providing massively increased choices. But they leave some groups nutritionally exposed, and erect barriers against increased consumption of vegetables and fruit. It is ironic that our post-modern society cannot manage the task that every less developed society has regarded as central – that of addressing the food needs of its members.

References

1   Mintel, March 1996. Reported in *The Guardian*, 27 March 1996.

2   Monopolies and Mergers Commission. 1995. *South West Water Services Ltd*. London: HMSO.

3   Cawley DP, Lee AJ, Lund PJ. 1994. *The Common Agricultural Policy and the UK Diet*. Paper presented at the *Food Policies and the Food Chain* conference, Reading, 19–21 September 1994. Based on a paper presented to the Committee on the Medical Aspects of Food Policy, 20 April 1994.

4   Department of Health. 1994. *Eat Well! An Action Plan from the Nutrition Task Force to Achieve the Health of the Nation Targets on Diet and Nutrition*. London: Department of Health.

5   Department of Health. 1996. *Eat Well II. A Progress Report from the Nutrition Task Force on the Action Plan to Achieve the Health of the Nation Targets on Diet and Nutrition*. London: Department of Health.

6   Low Income Project Team. 1996. *Low Income, Food, Nutrition and Health: Strategies for Improvement. A Report by the Low Income Project Team for the Nutrition Task Force*. London: Department of Health.

7   Neale RJ, Otte S, Tilson CH. 1995. Fruit: comparisons of consumption, attitudes, knowledge and preferences of primary school children in England and Germany. *Journal of Consumer Studies and Home Economics*; 19: 261–276.

8   Personal communication with Eric Booth, Soil Association, from Nutrition Task Force Low Income Project Team Working Group 2 – Policy (John Beaumont, Suzi Leather, Tim Lang and Clare Mucklow), May 1995.

9   Beck U. 1992. *Risk Society*. London: Sage.

10 Cox DN, Anderson AS, Lean MEJ, Mela D. 1995. Identifying barriers to increasing fruit and vegetable consumption in the UK: preliminary findings. *Appetite*; 24: 267.

11 Leather S. 1995. Fruit and vegetables: consumption patterns and health consequences. *British Food Journal*; 97: 7: 10–17.

12 Dobson B, Beardsworth A, Keil T, Walker R. 1994. *Diet, Choice and Poverty*. London: Family Policy Studies Centre.

13 Central Statistical Office. 1993. *Family Spending. A Report of the 1994-95 Family Expenditure Survey*. London: HMSO.

14 Personal communication with Deborah Lapthorne, Deprivation Officer, Plymouth Health Authority, 1994.

15 The Scottish Office. 1993. *The Scottish Diet. Report of a Working Party to the Chief Medical Officer for Scotland*. Edinburgh: The Scottish Office Home and Health Department/HMSO, Scotland.

16 European Commission. 1995. *The Agricultural Situation in the European Union 1994 Report*. Brussels/Luxembourg: European Commission.

17 Leather S. 1995. *Fruit and Vegetables: What are the Issues? Where are the Policies?* MAFF Consumer Panel Paper CP(95) 21/7. London: Ministry of Agriculture, Fisheries and Food.

18 Meat and Livestock Commission Press Office 1996.

19 Register: MEAL. *The Food Pocket Book*. 1994. London: NTC Publications Ltd.

20 Leather S. 1996. *Budgeting for Food on Benefits*. London: National Consumer Council.

Discussion: the gap between recommendations and current consumption

Simple, consistent messages

The need for simple and consistent messages to the general public cannot be over-emphasised. Research in the United States for the *5 A Day* programme indicated that those people who were aware of the need to eat five or more portions of fruit and vegetables were the people who are most likely to do so. The message needs to remain consistent with respect to how much fruit and vegetables to eat, that processed as well as fresh fruit and vegetables are included, and that the recommendation does not just apply to organically grown fruit and vegetables.

There is some confusion about the emphasis on figures in fruit and vegetable recommendations. Recommended intake targets in weights (for example 400g) are intended for discussion in the policy-making arena and are not intended to be part of the message to the general public.

It has also been suggested that the 'at least five a day' message places an over-emphasis on figures and that a simple message like 'you cannot eat enough' might be more appropriate. However, research indicates that quantified advice is important for consumers.[1] In view of this, the Nutrition Task Force chose to recommend at least five portions a day. Advice based on portions was considered preferable to advice based on weight, for two reasons. First, it is likely to be more meaningful for consumers, and secondly, the actual amounts of food eaten can vary greatly between, for example, people of different age groups. In the United States, the *5 A Day* campaign also emphasises the number of portions, although its message is now 'five or more' instead of 'eat five a day'.

Street-level barriers

There are a number of psychological, street-level barriers which act against fruit and vegetables. For example, some people may be put off by the perceived 'muddiness' of fruit and vegetables. When people want to buy a snack it may seem easier to go into a sweet shop than a greengrocer's. Other contributing factors include fruit not being wrapped, customers not being able to pick items of fruit individually, and the high cost of an individual piece of fruit in corner shops.

There is concern that supermarkets may have over-emphasised the importance of uniformity of fruit and vegetables, and it is encouraging to see more recent trends for supermarkets to sell varying sizes of fruit and vegetables.

Income and affordability barriers

The social class differences in fruit and vegetable consumption make the issues of low income and affordability important in any discussion about increasing consumption.

People need access to good quality, affordable fruit and vegetables – which raises issues of income, availability and access. Some of the barriers have been discussed by the Low Income Project Team of the Nutrition Task Force in England. In some areas of the UK, it is almost impossible to buy fresh vegetables of any quality. Recent surveys have also highlighted the price differential for consumers buying produce in supermarkets and those limited to local stores. In developing strategies, it is important to bear in mind that one-third of people in the UK do not have access to a car.

A key issue is that people on low incomes cannot necessarily afford to buy fruit and vegetables. For example, three-quarters of children in Glasgow are entitled to free school meals, which means that three-quarters of Glasgow parents cannot afford to buy their children's lunch. How can they be expected to provide five portions of fruit and vegetables a day?

There is a need to recognise that the market does sometimes fail and that changes will also be required at the supply level. One such change may be to reverse the trend which saw so many greengrocers' shops disappear in the 1980s. The Low Income Project Team identified 'shopping deserts' where low income groups do not have access to the range of fresh fruit and vegetables that other groups do.[2] As a result, the Institute of Grocery Distribution has initiated a project to develop facilities to improve provision to rural and inner city areas. One problem is that local stores have to charge high prices for produce because they do not benefit from the economies of scale that multiple retailers experience. This project aims to design a mobile shopping system which can offer those economies of scale.

What can be done to ensure that the market works for everyone, including those low income households where change is most needed? Large retailers could collaborate with local retailers or community food initiatives. At the same time, an official recognition that markets do sometimes fail is needed.

Lack of political will

Political will is needed to tackle the barriers to increasing fruit and vegetable consumption. In order to engender political will, policy makers need to be persuaded that it is in their interest to consider the interests of lower income groups, the so-called 'bottom third'. There is already political will to reduce expenditure on health care, so it may be possible to use fruit and vegetables as a focus for re-emphasising preventive health care. One way to help do this might be to give tax-payers more information on the costs of nutritional ill-health to tax-payers.

Another way is to bring political will from other spheres into nutrition. Food, for example, could be a focus for local economic regeneration, for reducing the Public Sector Borrowing Requirement, or as a vehicle for job creation.

A further suggestion for increasing political will is through practical illustrations of problems and potential solutions. For example, taking policy makers to visit shopping facilities in deprived areas can have a tremendous impact. Visits to farms engaged in innovative, local supply networks could be influential in illustrating ways forward. One such farm in Devon now employs 40 people, grows 85 plant varieties of fruit and vegetables and supplies 1,000 households within a 20-mile radius.

Establishing patterns early in life

Research indicates that consumption patterns are established early in life. Focus groups in the United States, organised as part of the *5 A Day* programme, found that those who ate more fruit and vegetables as children also ate more as adults. A study of men in North Karelia, in Finland, examined socioeconomic status in childhood.[3] Results showed that consumption of fruit and non-root vegetables, and consumption of vitamin C, were lower in people who were relatively deprived in socioeconomic terms in childhood, regardless of their adult socioeconomic status.

A survey of 1,200 school children and school meals in Glasgow found that only 22% of children selected fruit and 23% selected vegetables at their school meal.[4] In Finland, school meals are governed by nutritional standards and are given free to all pupils.

Children need to be a focus for increasing fruit and vegetable consumption, and various ways to ensure that such patterns are established in early life have been suggested. It is important to find ways of slotting fruit and vegetable consumption into the everyday structure of people's lives. One way might be through free or subsidised school fruit, giving all children the opportunity to have fruit every day. Another idea is to have public orchards in deprived areas, on the principle that any exposure to fruit and vegetables in people's own space for free is more likely to increase commercial use in time because it increases familiarity. Another finding of the US study was that when children had the autonomy to make their own choices, they did tend to eat more fruit and vegetables.

References

1   Cox DN, Anderson AS, McKellar S, Reynolds J, Lean MEJ, Mela DJ. In press. Consumer strategies for increasing fruit and vegetable consumption in the UK. Abstract. *Proceedings of the Nutrition Society.*

2   Low Income Project Team. 1996. *Low Income, Food, Nutrition and Health: Strategies for Improvement. A Report by the Low Income Project Team for the Nutrition Task Force.* London: Department of Health.

3   Lynch JW, Kaplan GA, Salonen JT. In press. Why do poor people behave badly? *Social Science and Medicine.*

4   Armstrong J. 1996. *A Survey of the Energy and Nutrient Composition and Choice of Fruit and Vegetables in School Meals Selected by a Sample of Schoolchildren in Strathclyde.* Thesis for a Master of Public Health. Glasgow: University of Glasgow.

Part 3

Strategies to close the gap: how policy makers, growers and retailers can contribute

Chapter 3

Vegetables and fruit: the effect of the Common Agricultural Policy

Jill Johnstone

National Consumer Council

Introduction

For more than 30 years, most agricultural production in the European Union has been governed by the Common Agricultural Policy (CAP). The origins of the CAP lie in the shortage of food: after the Second World War, under-supply of food was a major problem for Europe. The founding member states of the then Common Market placed a high priority on ensuring a stable and secure future for agriculture, both on employment and supply grounds. However, by the time the CAP came into being in the 1960s, agriculture had substantially recovered and the shortages had disappeared.

The CAP, including the fruit and vegetables regime which governs most fruit and vegetable produce, has traditionally relied on a number of procedures including guaranteed prices to farmers, quotas, high tariffs on imports, subsidies for exports, and withdrawal of food from the market. These procedures received increasing criticism as they resulted in higher prices, restricted consumer choice, and wastage of withdrawn produce.

The CAP was reformed in 1992 in order to address some of these problems. The fruit and vegetables regime was not reviewed until 1994, and reforms were made in 1996.*

The fruit and vegetables regime before 1996

The fruit and vegetables regime covers a whole range of fresh and processed fruits and vegetables, including most citrus and soft fruits and a range of fresh

---

*   The reforms to the fruit and vegetables regime were agreed in 1996, after the National Heart Forum expert meeting. However this Chapter includes some information about those reforms.

vegetables including cauliflower, tomatoes and lettuce. The main exceptions are potatoes, bananas, wine grapes, and peas and beans grown for fodder. All of these except potatoes are covered by other regimes.

Traditionally, the fruit and vegetables regime relied on three mechanisms:

- withdrawals
- quality standards, and
- import taxes and export subsidies.

Withdrawals

The CAP fruit and vegetables regime relied on aids to producer groups to control supplies and hence maintain prices, mainly through withdrawal of produce from the market. Producers who withdrew produce received a compensation payment at a level agreed at the farm price review. Produce withdrawn from the market was 'disposed of' in a number of different ways, including processing and distillation, free or subsidised produce for charities, or destruction of the food, usually by ploughing it back into the land.

Level of withdrawals

The level of withdrawals from the market varied considerably from year to year and between products – reflecting in the main the highly volatile nature of this market. Nevertheless, withdrawal from the market of more than one-third of total production was a fairly regular occurrence for some products – in particular lemons, some of the smaller orange varieties, and peaches and nectarines. In 1986–87 almost half of all lemons produced and almost 60% of mandarins were taken off the market. In 1992–93 almost a quarter of all peaches were withdrawn.

Table 1 *European Union fruit and vegetable withdrawals, 1982-93. Percentage of production withdrawn*

	1982–83	1984–85	1986–87	1989–90	1990–91	1992–93
Cauliflower	2.4	1.7	9.1	3.8	1.2	5.2
Tomatoes	0.7	0.3	8.4	0.4	0.9	1.6
Peaches	10.8	14.7	17.3	27.0	26.4	24.6
Lemons	19.8	6.1	47.8	10.3	1.3	5.5
Apples	13.4	9.0	4.8	1.0	1.2	15.6
Mandarins	5.7	4.5	58.6	5.3	2.7	2.2
Oranges	5.7	1.3	21.8	5.9	4.3	10.2
Nectarines				18.2	16.4	31.6

Source: See references 1 and 2.

Most of the fruit and vegetables withdrawn ended up either being destroyed, distilled into alcohol or fed to animals. Over the past 10 years, on average less than 2% of withdrawn fruit and vegetables was distributed to charities or other special need groups.

Quality standards

The fruit and vegetables regime laid down common quality standards for 37 types of fruit and vegetables. Despite their name, these quality standards were primarily market management tools (like quotas) aimed at keeping prices high without raising the budgetary cost of the regime. The total ban on retail sales of class 3 (that is, third-grade) produce, together with minimum size requirements for various fruit and vegetables, were justified by the European Union in terms of 'market transparency' and common standards. They had little to do with consumer protection. In its review of the regime in 1994, the Commission recognised that these standards are "ill perceived by consumers", depriving them "of produce suitable for consumption and traditionally consumed in their region".

Import taxes and export subsidies

Domestic prices were also supported through high import taxes and some quotas. In addition, large sums of money – about 200 million ecus (approximately £244 million) a year – were spent subsidising exports of fruit and vegetables.

Production of fruit and vegetables accounted for 16% of total agricultural output in 1990–92. Production trends for most products were increasing and, while consumption of processed produce (like fruit juice and frozen vegetables) was also increasing, for many fresh products the rate of increase was less than that of production. All the indications were that surpluses were becoming structural rather than seasonal.

The cost to tax-payers and consumers

The structure of the CAP meant that the public was paying twice over: once as tax-payers to support farmers through the CAP regime, and again as consumers through higher food prices in the shops.

The cost to tax-payers

In overall terms the fruit and vegetables regime accounted for relatively little of the CAP budget – between 3% and 5%. However, the 1993 figures showed a 77% increase in spending on fresh produce compared to 1992. For tax-payers, the regime represented very poor value for money. Much of the expenditure on fruit and vegetables was spent financing the destruction of edible, healthy and nourishing food. In 1993 almost one-third of the expenditure on this sector – 520 million ecus (approximately £635 million) - went on financing withdrawals from the market, most of which was destroyed or denatured.

There was an additional loss to tax-payers as a result of the high levels of fraud within the fruit and vegetables regime. A 1989 European Court of Auditors report on fruit and vegetable production[1] concluded that the system was "beset by fraudulent and irregular practices". Over the period 1983–87 the cost of uncovered frauds in the processing side of the regime alone was estimated to be over 85 million ecus (approximately £104 million).

The cost to consumers

The level of import taxes on a whole range of fruit and vegetables indicated that consumers were paying prices far in excess of those that could be achieved if the CAP price support system did not exist. For tomatoes the

European Union support price during the late 1980s was 270% higher than the world market price; for lemons the European Union price was more than double. The average 'tax' on imported tomatoes during that period was equivalent to 48p a pound.

The arrangements failed to ensure that consumers had access to the best quality produce. In particular, sub-standard produce could be subsidised for processing, while top quality fruit and vegetables were ploughed in or left to rot. The 1989 Court of Auditors report[1] estimated that in 1986–87 almost half a million tonnes of good quality lemons were withdrawn from the market and "for the most part destroyed" while up to 15% of the lemons which were processed were sub-standard. Lack of adequate monitoring and control mechanisms may at times have put consumers at risk. For example, the 1989 report found that currants which had been denatured for use as animal feed were later being sold for human consumption.

Finally, with the fruit and vegetables regime, farmers knew that they could get a payment for their produce regardless of whether there was a market demand for it. They therefore had much less inclination to think about the requirements of the market and to change their production accordingly.

Reform of the fruit and vegetables regime

The 1989 Court of Auditors report[1] highlighted a number of serious criticisms of the CAP regime:

- fraud and other 'irregularities' were commonplace

- the level of withdrawals, and what was done with this withdrawn produce, were a waste of tax-payers' money;

- quality standards were working against the consumer.

The report concluded that any "system which channels better quality produce for animal feed and for destruction, while reserving a lower quality for processing, is considered to be unacceptable".

In 1992 the then Agriculture Commissioner Ray MacSharry achieved a significant change in how the CAP works. The MacSharry reforms, which aimed to control production and to curtail surpluses, represented a shift from price support towards production controls and direct payments to farmers as compensation for the price support reductions.

However, fruit and vegetables were not included in the MacSharry reforms. Discussion since then led to reforms in 1996 and the introduction of new framework regulations on the common organisation of the market in fresh and processed fruit and vegetables. The aim of the new regime is to move European growers and processors of fresh fruit and vegetables towards a more market-oriented operation.

The main features of the new common organisation of the market are:
- revised levels of withdrawals, and
- a more prominent role for producer organisations.

Withdrawals

The reforms to the fruit and vegetables regime include alterations to the price support mechanism to discourage withdrawal, with a range of temporary aids to producers to ease the transition.

Market withdrawals are to be limited eventually to a yearly average of 10% of the total quantity of produce sold by each individual producer organisation. Community compensation for withdrawal is to be 20% less than the reference year (1995-96) in year one, falling to 40% less in year five.

Producer organisations

Producer organisations will be given a more prominent role under the reformed regime. The eligibility criteria for recognising provider organisations, and the rules for grower membership, will be more clearly drawn.

Grower members must market their entire production of relevant crops through the producer organisation but they may, with its authorisation, sell a small amount through farm shops or other marketing channels.

Producer organisations must set up an operational fund with contributions from their members. A European Union grant of 50% of eligible expenditure may be made to producer organisations on the basis of their operational programme. This will need to include elements to improve the quality of produce, orderly marketing, promotion of consumption, and environmentally sound production methods. In addition, a steadily reducing proportion of the funds of the producer organisations can be allocated to financing withdrawals from the market. The European Union funds must be matched by funds raised by grower members (the operational fund). Producer organisations or associations which are operating in more than one Member State are eligible for 60% funding.

In addition, the reforms make provision for a review of all the current arrangements with a view to preventing those for processed fruit and vegetables being used as an outlet for surplus production regardless of the potential marketability of it.

The effects of the reforms

Although the proposed reforms were widely discussed, it is as yet too early to say what impact they will actually have on fruit and vegetable consumption. The more market-oriented approach of the new fruit and vegetables regime could lead to improved promotion of fruit and vegetables. The greater degree of control given to producer organisations, and their responsibility for marketing, could both help to increase promotion activities. However, this depends on the organisations' competence and priorities, and on how they choose to use their increased control.

One concern is whether the increased power of the producer organisations will actually improve links between consumers and producers. To become members of a producer organisation, producers have to channel the majority of their produce through it. This may have the effect of creating monopolies and reducing the links between consumers and producers.

The GATT requirements on fruit and vegetables

Since July 1995, international trade in agricultural products has, for the first time, come under the world trade ground rules described in the General Agreement on Tariffs and Trade (GATT). These rules were agreed in 1994 by 117 countries with the aim of reducing subsidies and support for domestic producers.

Under GATT rules the European Union will have to replace taxes on imported produce with agreed tariffs. These will then have to be reduced by 36% overall by 2001, with a minimum reduction of 15% on the tariffs on all products. In 1990-91 this would have applied to one-third of the fresh fruit consumed in the European Union and 6% of the fresh vegetables. The GATT rules also require the European Union to reduce the export refunds which are used to subsidise European producers.

It seems likely that the changes introduced to the Common Agricultural Policy as part of the MacSharry plan will be largely sufficient to meet the GATT obligations without further cuts.

Conclusion and recommendations

The pre-1996 fruit and vegetables regime raised prices and denied consumers access to healthy products. Much of the expenditure on the regime went to finance the destruction of edible and nutritious food, and the regime was beset by fraud. Although the proposed reforms were widely discussed, it is as yet too early to say what impact they will actually have on fruit and vegetable consumption.

In its comments on the Commission's proposals for the reform of the fruit and vegetables regime, the National Consumer Council[3] argued that:

- There should be no monopoly role for producer organisations, as this might result in unreasonably high prices to consumers, poor quality and reduced choice. Farmers should not be forced to join producer organisations and sell their produce through them. Direct sales to retailers and consumers should be encouraged.

- The reduction in withdrawal prices, while welcome, does not go far enough. The reductions should be continued until subsidised withdrawals are phased out. If direct income support for producers is needed, it should not take the form of 'compensation for withdrawal' but should be targeted towards meeting specific social, environmental or structural objectives.

- Quality standards should not be set by the European Commission, but should be left to the market.

- Import taxes should be reduced and export funds phased out.

It remains to be seen whether the reforms introduced in 1996 will provide a better deal for consumers in the European Union.

References

1   European Commission. 1989. *Official Journal of the EC Information and Notices C128/89. Court of Auditors Special Report No 2/89 on the Organisation of the Markets in Fresh and Processed Fruit and Vegetables.* Luxembourg.

2   European Commission. Various years. *Agricultural Situation in the Community.* Luxembourg.

3   National Consumer Council. 1995. *Agricultural Policy in the European Union: The Consumer Agenda for Reform.* London: National Consumer Council.

Chapter 4

Vegetables and fruit: their place in national health strategies

Geoffrey Cannon

National Food Alliance

Introduction

The Health of the Nation, and other UK health strategies, can be seen as the most important initiatives in UK public health since the foundation of the National Health Service in 1947. They represent an acknowledgement that the government as a whole promotes the scientific consensus that prevention is a rational approach to major public health problems.

England

The Health of the Nation, the government's health strategy for England, set quantified targets for quantified time periods for heart disease, nutrition, obesity and smoking. The inclusion of diet and nutrition targets signalled the government's recognition that what we eat is important to the state of our health.

The Nutrition Task Force

To develop a strategy to achieve the targets, a national Nutrition Task Force was set up from 1992 to 1995. The Nutrition Task Force (NTF) included four constituencies: government, industry, health/medical organisations and consumer/public interest organisations. Several project teams were also established, in particular a Product Promotion Project Team to examine, among other things, the issue of fruit and vegetables:

> "The NTF recognises that if the targets for the reduction in the proportion of fat in the diet are to be met it will be necessary for people to increase the consumption of bread, pasta, rice and other cereal products, potatoes, fruit and vegetables and fish. It is proposed that a project team involving the Ministry of Agriculture, Fisheries and Food and the Department of Health, together with appropriate experts from the industry should carry out an analysis . . . [of the structure

and nature of the market for each of these sectors and of the] . . . levels of increase that might be possible, taking account of the barriers to increasing the market and increasing the supplies available . . ., following which the possible basis of a promotion campaign might be determined."[1]

The proposals of the Product Promotion Project Team

The Product Promotion Project Team produced a detailed report for analysing the structure and nature of the market and barriers to increased consumption. The report confirmed that the trends in domestic consumption, particularly for fresh or basic products, were static or declining, though consumption through the catering sector improved the picture for some products. Those products which showed encouraging signs of increased consumption were those which addressed consumers' desire for convenience, and the report noted that innovative developments in such products would be an important element in increasing consumption to the desired levels. The industry advised that there would be no difficulty in providing supplies to meet any foreseen increase in demand. The report also identified the barriers to increased consumption for each of the relevant products, and examined the current promotion activity of each of the sectors.

Proposal for a national media campaign

The report concluded that only a high profile media campaign would be likely to bring about the substantial changes in the diet that are required to increase consumption to the levels recommended. It emphasised that to have any lasting effect such a campaign would need to be sustained for a long period – at least three, and preferably five years – and recommended that the core of the campaign should be led and financed by government on a public information basis. The cost was estimated at £3-4 million a year. A commitment to supporting promotional activity from each of the sectors, from retailers and caterers, as well as support from educators and local community activity, was regarded as an essential part of the proposed campaign. In particular it was suggested that the sectoral interests were best placed to address specifically the identified barriers to increased consumption. The Project Team's report recommended an initial pilot project to test the feasibility and likely effectiveness of the proposals.

The Nutrition Task Force's response to the proposal

The Nutrition Task Force studied the report, but considered that any proposals for additional public expenditure should be fully justified. It therefore recommended that further work should be done to demonstrate the effectiveness and likely success of any proposed campaign to promote increased consumption of particular foods. This should include a systematic review to identify initiatives elsewhere and an evaluation of their nature and success.

It accepted the view of the Project Team that it would be essential for any campaign to be preceded by a pilot project, and recommended that if the government decided that a campaign might be justified, a steering group representing the main relevant interests should be set up to develop such a pilot project.

The government's response to the proposal

The government's response to the proposals for a high profile campaign was that it did not believe that this was the right approach: "It is for the relevant sectors to grasp the marketing opportunities presented by the quest for healthy eating to promote their products to the public."[2]

Scotland

The Scottish Diet Action Plan

In Scotland, a wide-ranging action plan for achieving the Scottish healthy eating targets by 2005, *Eating for Health – A Diet Action Plan for Scotland*,[3] was published in 1996. The emphasis is on a concerted approach, and the plan sets out recommendations for the different sectors of the food industry (producers, manufacturers, processors, caterers and retailers), the NHS, local authorities, community action, schools, the media and consumers. A number of the recommendations relate to fruit and vegetables, and the target of doubling fruit and vegetable intakes by 2005 is described as "the single most important dietary target".

The recommendations include further development of innovative initiatives and campaigns to stimulate Scottish demand for fruit and vegetables. Key steps include food producers stimulating consumer demand for vegetables and fruit by means of innovative developmental initiatives and imaginative marketing campaigns; the food manufacturing and processing industries developing, in consultation with the retailing sector, a wider range of products containing fruit and vegetables; caterers providing vegetables or side salads as part of the main course of every meal, within the price; and supermarkets considering innovative marketing techniques and pricing strategies to market fruit and vegetables.

Recognising the length of the process of change, the plan is, in effect, a blueprint for action over a decade.

Wales

In Wales, the issue of vegetables and fruit is gaining priority due to concerns about low levels of consumption. A working group on health gain targets, set up by the Chief Medical Officer for Wales, proposed targets for increased consumption of vegetables, salads and fruit among adults. These were under consultation at the time of publication of this report.

Northern Ireland

Since the National Heart Forum's expert meeting, Northern Ireland has also published a food and nutrition strategy, *Eating and Health – A Food and Nutrition Strategy for Northern Ireland*. This sets out dietary and nutritional targets, including a target for average consumption of at least five portions of fruit and vegetables each day, and action points for different sectors to help achieve the targets.

References

1   Department of Health. 1996. *Eat Well II. A Progress Report from the Nutrition Task Force on the Action Plan to Achieve the Health of the Nation Targets on Diet and Nutrition.* London: Department of Health.

2   Department of Health. 1996. *Government Response to the Recommendations from the Nutrition Task Force Report, Eat Well II.* London: Department of Health.

3   The Scottish Office. 1996. *Eating for Health – A Diet Action Plan for Scotland.* Edinburgh: The Scottish Office Department of Health/HMSO Scotland.

4   Food and Nutrition Strategy Group. 1996. *Eating and Health – A Food and Nutrition Strategy for Northern Ireland.* Belfast: The Health Promotion Agency for Northern Ireland.

Geoffrey Cannon is Chairman of the National Food Alliance and was a member of the Nutrition Task Force Product Promotion Project Team. He is also Science Director at the World Cancer Research Fund.

Chapter 5

Can UK producers meet an increase in demand for vegetables and fruit?

Michael Scott

National Farmers Union and Elgro

Introduction

The number of acres of land devoted to field vegetables in the UK has declined in recent years, partly due to improvements in technology which increase yields, and partly due to patterns of consumption.

Overall, consumption of vegetables has remained static for a number of years. There has been a fall in demand for traditional vegetables which can be produced in the UK climate, while demand for salads and exotic vegetables has increased.

The UK has a trade gap in salads and vegetables of £1 billion a year. Potatoes account for 15% of this, tomatoes 30%, lettuce, cucumbers and peppers 16%.

Several factors may account for the changes in consumption of vegetables. Changing lifestyles make consumption of traditional vegetables difficult as consumers tend to graze. Also, younger generations receive little or no formal education on how to prepare and cook vegetables and fruit.

The change in consumption patterns of different types of vegetables and fruit is the single most important factor to take into account when examining the UK growing industry's ability to accommodate any future increases in consumption.

Productive capacity

It is possible to achieve a significant increase in UK production of traditional vegetables and fruit. Developments in technology, particularly access to irrigation, have opened up whole areas of the UK to vegetable production.

Traditionally Lincolnshire and Kent provided the bulk of vegetables grown in the UK, but Suffolk, Norfolk, Cambridgeshire, Essex, the Midlands and Cornwall have become important producers. Access to adequate water supplies will become an increasingly important consideration. Other factors such as improved varieties particularly suited to UK conditions, and access to better fungicides, will also contribute.

An infrastructure of packhouses, transport systems and marketing already exists in the UK. However, the fragmentation of the industry has resulted in the development of many sophisticated and expensive packhouses, many of which are currently under-used and therefore uneconomic. An increase in consumption and throughput would be a major benefit to them.

The UK therefore has the ability to increase production, and the infrastructure in place to handle increased consumption of vegetables and fruit, but first it is necessary to change the eating habits of a nation.

Improving demand

There needs to be better coordination of the many current initiatives to inform people of the health benefits of vegetables and fruit.

Generic promotion of vegetables – that is general advice to the public to 'eat more vegetables' – is not the answer. If meaningful sums of money are available for crop-specific promotions, some success can be achieved. For example, a promotion of mushrooms in 1989 created a significant increase in demand, although it also resulted in a large increase in imports.

New methods of presenting vegetables must be found, to make them more attractive to today's consumers, and to ensure that they fit in with current lifestyles. Examples include floretted cauliflower and broccoli, or prepared sprouts presented in microwavable packs ready for cooking.

Also, the school curriculum needs to be adapted to ensure that children are aware of the benefits of consuming more vegetables and fruit and are able to prepare and cook them. Many young people leave school with very little knowledge of how to prepare and cook traditional vegetables. This is one area where a potential partnership could begin between government and the industry.

Funding the process

Any funds available to increase consumption of vegetables and fruit should be spent on promotion in its broader sense rather than on production. Funds are not required to aid production in an industry which is used to working in a free market.

Producers would support a coordinated, targeted approach to improving consumption over the medium to long term provided there was evidence that government, processors and retailers had committed funds. It is essential to include retailers in any such initiative, since they now account for 67% of all fresh vegetable sales in the UK.

Raising funds from the vegetable industry is a difficult task, due in part to the fragmented nature of the industry. However, the Horticultural Development Council has in place statutory levying powers to raise funds for research and development. If there were a long-term plan involving government, the industry and the retail sector, it would not be difficult to extend the Council's remit to include education and promotion.

The European dimension

The Common Agricultural Policy (CAP) fruit and vegetables regime was introduced in 1972 and has remained in place with some amendments (see Chapter 3),* with three elements:

1 Common quality standards
These are designed to keep sub-standard products off the market. In an ideal world they would allow cross-border trade at common pre-determined standards. The UK works to much higher standards in servicing the multiple sector: the top five retailers in the UK, and others, operate quality specifications which are an important element of the supply criteria.

2 Price and intervention systems
The objective of the price and intervention systems is to stabilise markets by establishing a floor price. Each year, basic prices are set for a number of products. If market prices fall below those prices, intervention can be triggered. In general the UK is against the policy of intervention; it is very difficult to achieve the objective of the policy and the system is fraught with fraud throughout Europe. However, there is a reluctance to abandon the system since it is now a part of what is effectively a social subsidy in many parts of southern Europe.

3 Reference prices
This is a system of levying a tax to deter non-European Union countries from dumping fruit and vegetables in Europe, if those products are also grown within Europe.

The expenditure allocated within the CAP budget for these activities, as related to UK fruit and vegetable production, is very small but can produce distortions. It used to be possible to grow certain crops with intervention as the target but that is no longer the case as far as vegetables are concerned. There are however citrus varieties which are full of pips and almost unsaleable, and which qualify for intervention. This cannot be right, and yet the system has been retained. All expenditure currently allocated to intervention should be redirected to increasing consumption.

There is nothing in the operation of the fruit and vegetables regime that would stand in the way of British farmers servicing a significant increase in demand for fruit and vegetables. These sectors have always operated with the

---

* The fruit and vegetables regime reforms were made after the National Heart Forum expert meeting took place. For information on the reforms, see Chapter 3.

minimum of support and interference from the CAP. It is a sector of agriculture that has been used to operating under the old fashioned laws of supply and demand.

The European Union has an interest in promoting greater consumption of fruit and vegetables and has established a fund to support initiatives, where it can be convinced that the sponsoring body accounts for a very significant proportion of overall production. The large mainland European co-operatives, in concert, can demonstrate this fact. However, the fragmented structure of the UK fruit and vegetables industry makes it difficult to access such funds in this country.

Conclusion

If a mechanism can be found to increase consumption of vegetables and fruit, with particular emphasis on the traditional varieties which can be produced in the UK's temperate climate, the fruit and vegetable industry has the capability to deliver increased production and the willingness to contribute financially along with all others involved in achieving the goal.

A national, well coordinated initiative is required, to bring together all interested parties. Generic advertising is not the answer. The main target for any initiative should be the chronically under-consuming age groups, and an educational programme should be devised as an interim measure. The help of the Department for Education and Employment in England, and its equivalents in other parts of the UK, should be enlisted to address the problem in schools. The Department of Health should spearhead the initiative. In this way government would be seen to be actively and effectively involved. Funds earmarked for such initiatives would convince all those involved in the production, processing and retail chain of the government's earnestness and would thereby encourage the necessary financial commitment.

If all these elements were in place, the farming base would be prepared to play its part both in terms of producing the goods and funding the long-term plans that would have a realistic chance of substantially increasing consumption of vegetables and fruit. It is a disgrace that the UK is almost the lowest in the European league for consumption of vegetables and fruit (see page 31).

At the time of the expert meeting, Michael Scott was Chairman of Elgro Ltd, a vegetable marketing company supplying the major multiples with fresh vegetables, the processing industry with fresh vegetables for freezing and chill meal production, and the wholesale markets.

Chapter 6

Retail strategies to increase demand for vegetables and fruit

Nigel Garbutt

Head of Research and Development, Safeway Stores plc

Introduction

This section looks at the strengths, weaknesses, opportunities and threats in terms of what the multiple retail sector can do to increase demand for fruit and vegetables.

Strengths

Perceived value for money

Large food retailers are perceived by the public as providing value for money. However, value for money is a complex equation between price-sensitivity, taste and flavour, and the physical appearance of the product. Supermarket data indicate that price is not the key factor in the debate about increasing consumption of fruit and vegetables. For example, Safeway's 'Savers' range of products are 'class 2' produce which meet the criteria for nutritional quality and freshness but are down-graded because of their appearance. While such products create an entry price point for the consumer, they have not increased overall consumption of the products. Therefore factors other than price have an important influence.

Freshness

Working closely with producers and growers, large retailers are able to establish a very short supply chain, with many products going from field to store in less than 24 hours. This, coupled with cool chain distribution, gives the product the freshness and shelf-life demanded by those customers who shop only once a week. This high degree of freshness helps preserve vitamin content, and consumers lose less to wastage.

Overnight distribution

Overnight distribution of fruit and vegetables has enabled large retailers to distribute fresh produce to all parts of the UK. Consumption of fruit and vegetables is increasing in Scotland, primarily, it seems, because of the availability of fresh produce at value-for-money prices.

The trusted ally

Consumers perceive that major retailers take food quality and safety seriously. Many retailers go further than legislation alone. For example, in terms of pesticide control, they are working with the National Farmers Union to develop integrated crop management standards which provide reassurance to consumers on the basic wholesomeness and safety of fresh produce.

Advanced marketing methods

Marketing methods are a major strength of the multiple retailers. The following methods are currently used to promote fruit and vegetables:

Offer of the week. 'Buy one, get one free' offers are very useful in driving up consumption at the beginning of the season.

Feature promotions. For example, 'orchard bins' at the supermarket entrance with inviting displays which encourage customers to try new varieties of fruit and vegetables.

Recipes. Information technology at the checkout can link various items together (for example items used in a promotional recipe) and give the customer a discount on those products.

Pairs of items. 'Pairs' of items are offered as a special promotion: for example strawberries and cream.

Multiple purchase discount. Purchasers get a discount when they buy a certain number of the same item.

In-store posters and leaflets. These are often displayed in the main store and also in places where customers are likely to be most receptive, for example in supermarket coffee shops and pharmacies.

In-store demonstrations and mobile kitchens. These allow customers to sample new and exotic fruit and vegetables and demonstrate how they can be used.

Weaknesses

The major food retailers face three significant challenges in relation to increasing consumption of fruit and vegetables. Firstly, there is a very low level of spend on 'above the line' marketing and promotion of fruit and vegetables. Secondly, consumers are confused by the plethora of symbols, schemes and leaflets about healthy eating. Messages to consumers must be clear and consistent. Thirdly, social classes IV and V are known to be less responsive to 'healthier' products.

Opportunities

Major retailers are in a position to offer consumers clear, uncomplicated and user-friendly messages that can be easily absorbed in the shopping environment. The scientific basis for these messages must of course be underpinned by research, and the government has an important role to play in giving clear guidance on the appropriateness of health claims for particular foods (see *Discussion* on page 104).

Retailers could plan more promotions around national events, to promote particular fruits and vegetables. For example, the Wimbledon tennis fortnight is very effectively used to promote sales of strawberries.

Retailers are exploring ways of improving the freshness and quality of fruit and vegetables: for example, new methods of packaging and presentation for prepared salads, which have a short shelf-life, but are popular due to their convenience, and new improved varieties of fruits and vegetables which offer better taste and flavour.

Advanced marketing techniques offer a major opportunity for promoting fruit and vegetables. Electronic point of sale (EPOS) data provide detailed information about people's buying habits, increasingly through the use of loyalty cards. This will enable retailers to target particular customers with literature which they are likely to be receptive to. It will also be possible in the future to recognise at the checkout purchasers who are not buying specific products (for example fruit and vegetables) and for the checkout technology to print customised discount vouchers. However, it is important that consumers do not perceive such methods as invasive.

Threats

There are two main threats to the successful promotion of fruit and vegetables by major retailers. Firstly, consumers receive many mixed messages about diet and health. For example, even though they perceive carrots to be a 'healthy' food, a media report about the levels of organo-phosphorous pesticides that carrots may contain can alarm consumers and significantly affect consumption levels. It is important to be careful and measured about what is communicated to consumers. Also, the popular press and campaigners should be encouraged to convey the concept of risk in a reasonable and balanced way.

Another threat is the decline of the family meal centre, as people graze and snack more.

By considering the strengths, weaknesses, opportunities and threats in terms of what the multiple retail sector can do, it should be possible to generate ideas for action on how to increase the consumption of fruit and vegetables.

Discussion: how policy makers, growers and retailers can contribute

Production

Growing the wrong kind of produce?

There is concern that growers may be growing the 'wrong kind' of vegetables and fruit. One problem for British growers is that the types of vegetables and fruit which are traditionally grown in the UK have a rather 'old-fashioned' image. This contrasts with the increasingly popular, less traditional varieties of 'exotic' fruit and vegetables which are usually imported. There is a substantial trade deficit in fresh vegetables in the UK, but many competitive countries, such as France, have no such deficit. British growers could be growing beans for baked beans, shallots, globe artichokes and more asparagus. Are UK producers being too conservative and growing the wrong types of vegetables?

Some growers have made considerable progress in expanding into less traditional vegetables and fruit in the UK. For example, in Cornwall there has been great success with growing broccoli and cauliflower, and this has greatly reduced the amounts of these vegetables imported from Brittany.

However, there are practical difficulties for UK producers growing 'exotic' fruit and vegetables. Other countries can often grow this type of produce at significantly lower prices than are possible in the UK. For example, the harvesting of mangetout and sugar snap peas cannot be done at prices that are competitive with countries like Zimbabwe or Guatemala. Courgettes, which are increasing in popularity in the UK, can be grown outside in the UK climate only within a very short window of time. So, while some growers in Devon may have been successful growing courgettes, others in Lincolnshire have gone bankrupt in the process. The attractions of growing cereals under the Common Agricultural Policy (CAP) compared with the risks involved in these niche markets are a real factor discouraging expansion in these types of produce.

Common Agricultural Policy issues

Much concern has been expressed about the wastage of fruit and vegetables under the CAP. A great deal of the produce going into intervention was destroyed under the traditional fruit and vegetables regime of the CAP. This has been particularly true of citrus fruits, apricots and peaches. The fruit and vegetables regime, at least until its reform in 1996 (see Chapter 3), gave no incentive to grow what consumers wanted, a situation which is likely to remain until there is a shift from production-support based mechanisms to market-based incentives. There is a view that, regardless of how much it is in need of reform generally, the CAP as it stands is not in itself a barrier to increasing fruit and vegetable consumption in the UK.

However, it is essential to consider all aspects of the CAP, and not just the fruit and vegetables regime in isolation. The effect of the CAP on the supply and relative pricing of other products also impacts on fruit and vegetable consumption (see page 43).

There is concern about the lack of nutritional considerations in the CAP and agricultural policy in general. The CAP was drawn up in the 1960s, based on objectives relating to the supply of food and the perceived needs for food. Under Article 129 of the Maastricht Treaty on public health, other Directorates in the European Commission, such as the Agriculture Directorate, now have to include 'health protection requirements' in their policies. This will apply to any future reforms of the CAP.

Another factor contributing to the wastage under the CAP may be production methods. For example, the use of nitrates can result in a high uptake of water which can lead to flavourless vegetables. This is one possible reason why vegetables are not popular with consumers.

Use of technology

Some of the barriers to increasing vegetable and fruit consumption might be overcome with technology. For example, the new, genetically manipulated tomato requires less water and has an improved flavour. Brussels sprouts are often rejected by consumers because they lose their texture when cooked, and their high sulphur content can result in flavours which some consumers find unacceptable. Scientists are working to understand the metabolic pathways which lead to these flavours and to the loss of texture. Genetic manipulation would be one way of tackling these problems.

There are, however, grave concerns about the use of technology as a tool to increase vegetable and fruit consumption and producers are likely to encounter consumer resistance to this approach. This could apply, for example, to increased use of agro-chemicals or to genetic manipulation. There is a danger that, if vegetable and fruit production goes in the direction of genetic manipulation, consumers will be turned off rather than encouraged to increase their consumption.

Despite consumer concerns about biotechnology, care should be taken not to dismiss any real benefits to consumers. For example, processing technology can be used to add novelty and convenience to vegetables and fruit – in the form of manufactured products – which can make them more attractive to some consumers. Threats need to be turned into opportunities, to find food manufacturing processes and novel ideas which can make produce more attractive.

Distribution

Shift towards local supply systems

Supermarkets are often urged to shift towards encouraging local supply and taking their produce from small local growers. Increased emphasis on local supply networks would contribute to decreasing the number of 'food miles', which would be beneficial from an environmental and sustainability perspective. Ideally, a shift in agricultural policy would be accompanied by a shift in supermarket policy to take a 'look towards our land' approach, with more social responsibility.

Supermarkets recognise the economic sense of encouraging local producers. Local growers supplying Safeway, for example, can deliver into any of six regional distribution centres. Multiples have also collaborated with regional initiatives – such as the *Taste of the West* campaign – which promoted locally grown produce. Another initiative, *The Initiative on Food Marketing*, is designed to help reduce the trade deficit. This initiative brings the different sectors of the agricultural and food industry together so that more fresh produce from local agricultural and horticultural enterprises in the UK can be sourced.

Fewer out-of-town stores

Following intervention by the Secretary of State for the Environment in response to a request from the Royal Commission on Environmental Pollution, fewer out-of-town stores are being built, and some supermarkets are now developing and re-vamping city centre stores.

Problems with distribution networks to non-supermarket outlets

The vast majority of current distribution networks are set up to serve the large supermarkets. Currently around two-thirds of produce is sold through supermarkets and this figure is likely to move towards 80% in the next few years.

Those people who do not shop at supermarkets are likely to face increasing problems with access to vegetables and fruit. Distribution to outlets other than supermarkets has traditionally been done on a low cost basis, straight from farms into wholesale distribution points. As this sector continues to decrease, distribution networks will increasingly concentrate on supply to supermarkets at the expense of supplying non-supermarket outlets. It is a problem to work out how that sector is going to be served.

Promotion

Extended role for the Horticultural Development Council

There is potential scope for extending the Horticultural Development Council's remit and statutory levy to include education and promotion of fruit and vegetables. This move is more likely to be welcomed by growers if funding is matched by government. Such government funding would function as a signal to the growing fraternity that the levy would be used for educational and promotional work. However, there is virtually no possibility of securing further *voluntary* funding from growers. The horticultural industry, however, might agree to changing the basis of the statutory levy if this was to fund a coordinated three- to five-year programme to promote fruit and vegetables.

Whether the remit of the Horticultural Development Council (HDC) could be extended to become a marketing body, akin to the Meat and Livestock Commission, is uncertain. The HDC was put in place in response to the government's withdrawal of near market research (product-related research or research on marketing and promotion) from horticulture, and raises £3.5 million a year for such research. It does seem possible, however, that the remit could be extended to include education and promotion, given government support.

Part 4

Promoting vegetables and fruit: UK and international interventions

Increasing vegetable and fruit consumption: interventions to change attitudes and improve access

Ann Foster

Scottish Consumer Council

Karen McColl

Consultant

Introduction

There are many barriers which inhibit an increase in fruit and vegetable intakes and various strategies have been designed to address these barriers. Some interventions have sought to improve access to fruit and vegetables by tackling barriers such as cost and availability. Other interventions, both large and small scale, aim to increase fruit and vegetable intakes by changing attitudes. Despite conflicting evidence on the impact of attitudes on behaviour, studies suggest that it is possible to increase fruit and vegetable intakes with this approach.

Research into Scottish attitudes to fruit and vegetable consumption suggests that there is a need for quantitative guidance on increasing fruit and vegetable intakes.

Some strategies for change are clearly easier for consumers than others and these need to be promoted. Research also suggests that strategies should be carefully targeted. This process should take into account the beliefs and readiness to change of the target group.

Perceived barriers to change

Research into Scottish eating patterns and attitudes towards fruit and vegetables found that less than half of the sample were meeting the World Health Organization recommendation for 400g, or five portions, of fruit and vegetables (excluding potatoes) per day.[1] Over half of those with a low intake of fruit and vegetables (less than two portions) said they felt they were eating the right amount of vegetables and 24% felt they were eating the right amount of fruit. The results of this research, funded by the Scottish Office and carried out by the Scottish Consumer Council and the Department of Human Nutrition at the University of Glasgow, suggest that most Scottish people consider that they have a healthy diet because they eat 'some' fruit and vegetables. This complacency about the need to increase fruit and vegetable intakes highlights the need for quantitative guidelines and lends support to the 'at least five a day' strategy.

The same research also explored the barriers to fruit and vegetable consumption. Respondents were asked to agree or disagree with a number of statements which described perceived barriers to eating more fruit and vegetables (see Table 1). Two perceived barriers were prominent for fruit: it is expensive and does not make a filling snack. Several perceived barriers for vegetables were important: doubts about the nutritional value of frozen or tinned vegetables, cost, limited ways of serving vegetables, and their lack of taste appeal. The fact that children do not like vegetables was also an important factor for respondents with children. For both fruit and vegetables, a very high proportion of respondents disagreed with the perceived barrier that they 'are not readily available'.

Table 1 *Agreement on perceived barriers to increasing fruit and vegetable intakes in a survey of 1,011 Scottish adults*

Perceived barrier	Percentage agree	Percentage disagree
Fruit		
Fruit is too expensive to buy much more of nowadays	38	49
Fruit does not make a filling snack	30	61
My spouse/partner does not like fruit	6	59
I do not really have the opportunity to eat much fruit	7	88
My children do not like fruit	4*	70*
Fruit is not readily available	5	92
Vegetables		
I would eat more vegetables if frozen or tinned vegetables were as good as fresh	27	59
Vegetables are too expensive to buy much more of nowadays	22	63
You are limited to the ways that you can serve vegetables during the day	22	64
I would eat more vegetables if they tasted better	20	71
My children do not like vegetables	18*	53*
My spouse/partner does not like vegetables	4	59
Vegetables are difficult to prepare	4	88
Vegetables are not readily available	4	93

* As a percentage of respondents with children.

Source: See reference 2.

Research by the Health Education Authority (HEA)[3] explored attitudes to fruit and vegetables in qualitative research in 1991. The findings suggest that consumers classify fruit and vegetables into three distinct categories: fruit, vegetables and salad. Of these, fruit is the most acceptable group and is seen as 'attractive', 'portable' and 'good for you'. Salad is almost as popular and was described as 'crunchy', 'quick to prepare', 'cool and refreshing'. Traditional vegetables hold least appeal and are seen as 'boring', 'bland' and 'inconvenient'.

Further research by the HEA, as part of its 1994 omnibus survey, quantitatively explored attitudes to fruit and vegetables and perceived barriers.[4] Twenty-one per cent of respondents thought that fruit was too expensive. Nineteen per cent of respondents felt that vegetables were time-consuming to prepare, and 18% that they were too heavy to carry; 13% said they thought that they were too expensive. Sixty-five per cent of respondents believed that people did not know enough about preparing and cooking vegetables. Twenty-four per cent of respondents said that fruit and vegetables did not fill them up as much as other foods.

The HEA's qualitative research reinforced the fact that consumers are confused about the benefits of frozen or processed fruit and vegetables compared to fresh. Fresh fruit and vegetables are widely perceived as more healthy than frozen varieties.

Interventions to increase fruit and vegetable consumption

Interventions to increase fruit and vegetable consumption may adopt several different approaches. They may be concerned with helping people overcome any combination of the barriers outlined above. For example, many interventions aim to improve access to fruit and vegetables in various settings, while others aim to change attitudes to fruit and vegetable consumption.

In 1995 researchers at the Institute of Food Research in Reading and the Department of Human Nutrition at the University of Glasgow conducted a MAFF-funded intervention study.[5] One of the main objectives of the study was to identify specific practical strategies that people used to attain the recommended five portions a day.

Three groups of people were identified at each site. Two of these groups, A and B, took part in the intervention. A control group C was also recruited. Features of the intervention included:

- attendance at a 'fruit and veg for health' lecture

- explanation of definitions of fruit and vegetable portions

- recipes for and tasting of vegetable-based dishes

- charts for recording measures, and

- lunch boxes and fridge magnets.

Groups A and C weighed all their food for seven days in a baseline study, and did so again in weeks 4 and 8 of the study. Group B did not weigh their food, but recorded it with descriptive tools.

Results from the study of weighed food showed that fruit and vegetable intake increased significantly from baseline at week 4 and week 8 in Group A, but this did not happen in the control group.

The intervention study groups (A and B) were then divided into those who achieved and those who did not achieve five portions a day. The main differences in strategies between those groups were that the achievers found the following approaches easier than did the non-achievers: eating fruit as a dessert, two portions of vegetables with a meal, fruit as a snack between meals, fruit as a starter, or having two portions of fruit with a meal.

These are simple, everyday approaches indicating that it is not necessary to become vegetarian to achieve these recommendations and that simple, everyday methods are effective. Overall the easiest strategy was drinking fruit juice, with no difference between the groups. The next easiest strategies were eating fruit as a dessert, having two portions of vegetables with a meal, and fruit between meals as snacks. Other strategies – such as having a bowlful of salad with a meal, or chopped fruit with breakfast cereal, choosing new fruit or vegetables for variety, replacing a meat dish with a vegetable dish, or eating home-made soup – showed no differences between achievers and non-achievers.

This research suggests that it is possible to increase fruit and vegetable intakes to achieve the current recommendations. It is clear that people perceive some strategies as easier than others and these need to be identified and promoted, preferably with quantitative guidelines.

Research in Scotland explored the support for a range of potential promotional incentives to encourage consumption of fruit and vegetables.[1] Table 2 outlines the incentives described in the survey and the degree of support for each.

Table 2 *Percentage of respondents rating promotional incentives to encourage consumption of fruit and vegetables as a very good idea or a good idea*

Promotional incentive	Very good idea	Good idea
Reduce price of fruit and vegetables in the shops	51	36
Emphasise the importance of eating fruit and vegetables for health reasons	42	49
Use special offers such as 'Buy five, get one free'	33	43
Give better information on what is needed per day	29	52
Encourage people to eat more fruit and vegetables by advertising	25	53
Give better information on what represents a portion on packs of fruit and vegetables	23	51
Use a leading sports personality to promote fruit and vegetable consumption	13	35

Source: See reference 1.

All of the ideas received reasonable support from respondents except the use of a leading sports personality to promote fruit and vegetables. The most popular incentive – reducing the price of fruit and vegetables in shops – was targeted at the perceived cost barrier. Similarly, the option with the third highest level of support was the use of special offers such as 'Buy five, get one free' for fruit. On the other hand, the second most popular approach – to emphasise the importance of eating fruit and vegetables for health reasons – was based on provision of information and change of attitudes.

Another study, for the Health Education Board for Scotland, found that participants in eight focus group discussions were well informed about healthy eating and that what was lacking was incentive rather than an understanding of the logistics of healthy eating.[6] Healthy eating suffered from the negative associations of being restrictive, unappetising, insubstantial and extreme. Fruit, vegetables and salad were considered unappetising and insubstantial.

The study also described a generally fatalistic attitude to healthy eating which manifested itself differently in young and older respondents. Younger respondents could see no real need to change since they felt healthy and had experienced no negative effects. Older respondents, however, appeared to consider that it was too late to change, having eaten 'the wrong foods' for years. The study also suggested that some people were eating more healthily than they might believe. Respondents appeared to be conditioned by the concepts of healthy eating as a strict regime and the mythology of the poor Scottish diet. That is, people could identify with foods which are repeatedly highlighted as examples of the Scottish diet – chips, fried foods and so on – whether or not they were eaten occasionally or every night.

Interventions to improve access to fruit and vegetables

There have been a variety of interventions, often at local level, aimed at improving access to fruit and vegetables. These interventions have attempted to tackle potential barriers such as the cost or limited availability of fruit and vegetables and have taken place in a variety of settings. For example, the Bain Club enterprise in Edinburgh has tried to improve availability of fruit and vegetables in primary schools, sheltered housing schemes and community centres by initiating mobile fruit and vegetable shops. The Barri Grub project promotes fruit and vegetables to schools and community groups through its mobile shop. The Jeely Piece Club in Castlemilk in Glasgow, funded by Glasgow City Council, gives children fresh fruit at lunchtime. The former Highland Regional Council funded the introduction of a high-tech version in their schools in the form of a Smart Card scheme which rewards children with points for healthy choices.

Another way in which projects attempt to improve access to fruit and vegetables is through community agriculture or horticulture schemes. These schemes reduce the number of links in the chain between growers and consumers in order to reduce costs and eliminate profit margins. Examples of this type of scheme include the Edinburgh Community Project, the home produce scheme of Argyll and the Islands Enterprise, and the East Finland Berry and Vegetable project. The latter, as part of the North Karelia study, attempted to increase the production and marketing of berries and vegetables in Finland.

The Govan Healthy Eating Project aims to reduce the costs of healthy eating and redirects the profits normally made on milk tokens back into the community as a 'healthy eating dividend' of fruit or vegetables. Similarly, the Dalmarnock Food Coupon scheme in Glasgow distributed 'money off' coupons for healthy foods such as fruit and vegetables.

Many co-operatives aim to reduce the costs of and to improve access to fruit and vegetables. These co-operatives involve groups of people operating collectively to bulk buy fruit and vegetables at lower costs. Some co-operatives also deliver the produce to people who have difficulty in getting to supermarkets, greengrocers or markets.

In the workplace setting, a study in Minnesota attempted to tackle the barriers of cost and availability of fruit and salad in an office cafeteria.[7] During the three weeks of the intervention there were more choices for fruit and salad ingredients and their prices were cut by half. In that time, purchases of fruit and salad increased three-fold compared to the baseline study. After the intervention stopped, purchases of fruit and salad dropped again, but not to baseline levels.

In many projects to increase fruit and vegetable intakes, there is incomplete monitoring or evaluation. Larger studies which attempt to increase fruit and vegetable intakes by changing attitudes tend to have more comprehensive evaluation procedures.

Interventions to change attitudes to fruit and vegetables

Information strategies based on changing attitudes and/or beliefs are numerous. There is some conflicting evidence on the impact of attitude changes on behavioural change. Not all people who know about the health benefits of a healthy diet and who are fully capable of putting it into practice actually choose to do so.

Health promotion theories describe models which attempt to explain health behaviour and explore the relationship between attitudes and behaviour. The Health Belief Model, for example, suggests that individuals may become ready to eat more fruit and vegetables if they are aware of the benefits of fruit and vegetables and consider themselves to be susceptible to coronary heart disease and cancer. Using the Health Belief Model, Dittus et al studied the relationship between attitudes and consumption of fruit and vegetable intakes in a survey of 1,069 adults in Washington state.[8] Analysis of the results by multiple regression suggested that attitudes account for only 16% of the variance in fruit and vegetable intakes. Barriers to fruit and vegetable intakes were the largest component of the variability. It is worth noting, however, that the barriers included a "disbelief that fruit and vegetables have cancer-preventing attributes" as well as concerns about cost, agrochemicals and how to prepare fruit and vegetables. The authors concluded that nutrition educators should "concentrate on identifying the barriers to behaviour change and developing suggestions to circumvent them".

The Transtheoretical Model for health behaviour suggests that people experience various stages of readiness for change. The likelihood of a person responding to health promotion strategies depends on their stage of change. Laforge et al explored the stages of change in relation to the *5 A Day* campaign in the United States.[9] People who are in the 'precontemplation' stage, for example, are not eating the recommended amount of fruit and vegetables, nor have they any intention to do so. The authors suggest that 'precontemplators' should be targeted with a different approach, including more information about the benefits of fruit and vegetables. This type of approach would be more appropriate than the action-oriented approach for people in other stages of readiness to change.

This idea is reflected in the results of a study in North Carolina which compared the effects of computer nutrition messages which were tailored to an individual's stage of change and health beliefs with messages which were not tailored.[10] The intervention aimed to reduce fat intake and increase fruit and vegetable intakes. Significant decreases in total fat and saturated fat intakes were observed in the group with the tailored messages compared with the control group. Fruit and vegetable consumption, however, did not increase in either group.

In general, research supports the idea that promotional strategies should adapt to take into account the stage of change of the target group. The barriers to change mentioned above may be different for people at varying stages of readiness to change. The primary barrier facing someone who has no intention of eating more fruit and vegetables – a so-called precontemplator – may be that they do not know about the potential health benefits of fruit and vegetables. An information strategy which explains the health effects may be more appropriate for this person than a campaign exploring new and exciting ways to prepare fruit and vegetables. Someone who is already aware of the health arguments and says that they do intend to eat more fruit and vegetables, however, would benefit little from the informational approach. The barriers facing this person (relating to cost, availability or preparation ideas) are different, so the strategy must also be different.

This may sound like common sense. However, it does illustrate that intervention strategies aimed at increasing fruit and vegetable intakes by changing attitudes must be carefully targeted and tailored to the target group. Lack of information and attitudinal factors must be considered in the context of other barriers to fruit and vegetable consumption.

There are encouraging results from studies in this area. In the *2 Fruit 'n' 5 Veg Every Day* campaign, a collaborative, multi-sectoral project to promote fruit and vegetable consumption in Victoria, Australia,[11] one in four people said they had tried to increase the total amount of fruit and vegetables they ate, and about one in five said that they actually increased the total amount of fruit and vegetables they ate as a direct result of the campaign. The proportion of respondents eating more than five servings of vegetables a day increased from 11% at baseline to 16% at the end of phase 3.

The project, which began in 1992, involved a wide range of media, educational and community activities and sponsorship deals (see Table 3). In 1995 six out of ten adults in Victoria were aware of the *2 Fruit 'n' 5 Veg Every Day* slogan and awareness of the campaign was high. Despite the increase in consumption of fruit and vegetables, 84% of adults in Victoria are still eating less than the recommended amount of vegetables and 90% are eating less than the recommended two fruit and five vegetables every day, suggesting that there is still a need to promote both vegetables and fruit.

Table 3 *Activities included in the '2 Fruit 'n' 5 Veg Every Day' campaign strategy, Victoria, Australia*

Strategy	Activity
Point of sale material	Promotional material for supermarkets and fresh produce stores. *Snack 'n' Pack* cookbook, recipe cards, posters, balloons, stickers etc.
Community	Kit sent to health professionals, community health centres, local government. Additional resources available including T-shirts, aprons, tea towels.
Catering	Kit sent to catering outlets, hospitals, workplaces and educational institutions.
Schools	Activity booklet with ideas for classroom and other campaign activities sent to schools. Competitions held for primary and secondary school students.
Sponsorship	Sponsorship of various sporting bodies.
Media/PR	TV and radio advertisements, features and interviews. Press advertising. Tram and bus advertising. Newspaper competition. Radio promotions including fruit and vegetable hampers as give-aways and/or competition prizes.

Source: See reference 11.

Conclusion

Research indicates that it is possible to increase fruit and vegetable intakes to achieve the current recommendations. Clear and simple strategies need to be identified and promoted, preferably with quantitative guidelines. In addition, research suggests that strategies should be carefully targeted and should address the beliefs, readiness to change and barriers to change of the target group.

References

1   Anderson AS, Lean MEJ, Foster A, Marshall D. 1994. Ripe for change: Fruit and vegetables in Scotland – current patterns and potential for change. *Health Bulletin*; 52(1): 51–64.

2   Marshall D, Anderson A, Lean M, Foster A. 1994. Healthy eating: Fruit and vegetables in Scotland. *British Food Journal*; 96: 7: 18–24.

3   Health Education Authority. 1991. *Fruit and Vegetable Development. Qualitative Research.* Unpublished report.

4   Health Education Authority. 1994. *Omnibus Survey on Healthy Eating.* Unpublished report.

5   Cox DN, Anderson AS, McKellar S, Reynolds J, Lean MEJ, Mela DJ. In press. Consumer strategies for increasing fruit and vegetable consumption in the UK. Abstract. *Proceedings of the Nutrition Society.*

6   Report prepared by System Three Scotland for the Health Education Board for Scotland. 1993. *Qualitative Research on Healthy Eating Promotional Materials.* Edinburgh: Health Education Board for Scotland.

7   Jeffery RW, French SA, Raether C, Baxter JE. 1994. An environmental intervention to increase fruit and salad purchases in a cafeteria. *Preventive Medicine*; 23: 788–792.

8   Dittus KL, Hiller VA, Beerman KA. 1995. Benefits and barriers to fruit and vegetable intake: Relationship between attitudes and consumption. *Journal of Nutrition Education*; 27: 120-126.

9   Laforge RG, Greene GW, Prochaska JO. 1994. Psychosocial factors influencing low fruit and vegetable consumption. *Journal of Behavioural Medicine*; 17: 4: 361–374.

10 Campbell MK, DeVellis BM, Strecher VJ, Ammerman AS, DeVellis RF, Sandler RS. 1994. Improving dietary behaviour: the effectiveness of tailored messages in primary care settings. *American Journal of Public Health*; 84: 5: 783-787.

11 Stafford H. 1995. *Progress Report: Evaluation of Phase II of the Victorian 2 Fruit 'n' 5 Veg Every Day Campaign.* Victoria: Food and Nutrition Program, Deakin University, Australia.

Chapter 8

5 A Day – for Better Health: lessons from the United States

Gloria Stables

5 A Day Program Director, National Cancer Institute, United States

Jerianne Heimendinger

Research Scientist, AMC Cancer Research Center, United States

Introduction

Over the past decade, consensus on the scientific basis for dietary change has grown steadily. Seminal publications include Doll and Peto's *The Causes of Cancer,*[1] the National Cancer Institute's *Cancer Control Objectives for the Nation: 1985–2000,*[2] *The Surgeon General's Report on Nutrition and Health,*[3] *Diet and Health: Implications for Reducing Chronic Disease Risk,*[4] *Healthy People 2000: National Health Promotion and Disease Prevention Objectives,*[5] and *Nutrition and Your Health: Dietary Guidelines for Americans.*[6]

These reports provided the basis for consistent policy-making in diet and health issues in the United States, and have enabled national, state and local governments to implement nutrition programmes which address national goals. Specifically for fruit and vegetables, the scientific evidence linking fruit and vegetable consumption to cancer prevention has grown dramatically.[7-13]

In 1991, the National Cancer Institute (NCI) launched the national 5 A Day programme – a major population-based public health initiative for nutrition and cancer,[14] based on this scientific evidence and a tested state-based prototype.[15]

Description of the 5 A Day programme

The 5 A Day programme is a national partnership between the fruit and vegetable industry, represented by the Produce for Better Health Foundation (PBH) and the NCI. This partnership has a vision for modifying national dietary behaviours, using the scientific credibility of the NCI and the ability provided by industry to reach the entire US population.

The *5 A Day* programme aims to communicate its message through the mass media, government, industry, community channels, and research efforts. Using social marketing techniques and theory-based strategies, the NCI and PBH work together to develop, implement and evaluate a variety of interventions. The major programme components are:

- mass media

- reinforcement at point of sale

- state and community components, and

- research and evaluation.

The national media campaign is designed to increase public awareness of the *5 A Day* message and communicate the skills-building information needed to encourage Americans to eat more fruit and vegetables.

The national programme facilitates partnerships and ensures consistent execution of the *5 A Day* message by setting standards and establishing agreements with all partners participating in the programme. The NCI has licensed all 50 state and four territorial health departments as the health authority to organise state-level *5 A Day* programmes, and it has delegated to the PBH the authority to license industry partners. National programme guidelines have been developed for a variety of partners such as the health departments, supermarkets, restaurants, food services, merchandisers and suppliers.[16]

By 1996, 1,200 industry partners, including retailers (with chains representing over 30,000 supermarkets nationwide), state and federal agricultural commodity boards, branded companies, wholesalers, merchandisers, suppliers, and food services were licensed to participate. The purpose of the retail component of the programme is to reach consumers with information and motivational messages at the point of purchase. The retailers and their suppliers participate in *5 A Day* by displaying promotional materials and the *5 A Day* logo on eligible products, incorporating the *5 A Day* message in print and broadcast advertisements, developing interactive events such as taste tests and store tours in supermarkets, and resource-sharing with the community component through the state *5 A Day* coalitions. Restaurants and food service operators are recent additions to the point of sale component.

The programme is supported by intervention research and nationwide evaluation (see page 93).

Funding

Initial funding for the *5 A Day* programme came from the Produce for Better Health Foundation, which contributed $500,000 to the programme in the first year and made media contributions (broadcast time and space for print advertising). In addition NCI spent $400,000 in the first year of the programme.

Over the past five years, the fruit and vegetable industry has spent approximately $150 million on the *5 A Day* programme, on advertising and on in kind donations to state and local coalitions. The NCI has spent an estimated $25 million, primarily on behavioural change research and on media and communications. The state health departments and other state government agencies have also made substantial contributions, although it is hard to estimate these in financial terms. For example, health departments provide overall state coordination, the departments of agriculture encourage local produce sold through farmers' markets, and state departments of education have adapted the *5 A Day* message for the school nutrition education curriculum. The US Department of Agriculture WIC (women, infants and children) programme also promotes the *5 A Day* message through education materials and interventions.

Public/private partnerships

Use of a public/private partnership as the mechanism to formulate and disseminate the *5 A Day* message is one of the essential features of the National *5 A Day* programme.

Development of the national partnership between the NCI and the fruit and vegetable industry was made possible by the formation of the Produce for Better Health Foundation, a non-profit consumer education organisation representing the highly diverse fruit and vegetable industry. Made up of thousands of companies, PBH represented the first time that the fruit and vegetable industry had collaborated on such a large scale with a health partner towards a common, consumer marketing objective that embraced fresh, frozen, canned and dried products.

The prototype California *5 A Day* campaign had demonstrated the feasibility of a state health agency working in partnership with agriculture boards and commissions, branded fruit and vegetable companies, and supermarkets to deliver large-scale interventions with modest government resources, as well as the existence of substantial interest in participation by states and industry groups outside California.[14] With the formation of PBH, it became feasible to elevate the partnership to a national level.

The agreement between the NCI and PBH calls for the NCI to serve as the programme's scientific voice to the public, to secure health and government partners, to conduct evaluation, and to advance intervention research. The PBH's role is to facilitate implementation of the programme in the food industry, to work with the NCI to develop guidelines and programme direction, to ensure that programme standards are maintained by industry partners, and to assist with evaluation.

Together, the NCI and PBH provide nationwide leadership, an infrastructure, and a template for action that can be transferred to state and local levels. Nationally, the NCI and PBH conduct market research, develop promotional themes and materials, and generate publicity to support the activities of all partners. At the state and local levels, therefore, partners can build on these to organise and run complementary interventions with regional or locally relevant 'hooks'. As the programme matures, additional collaborations with other national organisations, such as the American Dietetic Association (ADA) are being established. In this case, the ADA will use its consumer hotline and media spokespersons to reach consumers, and will also urge its 65,000 members to implement *5 A Day* activities in their work settings. This three-tiered approach of complementary national, state and local roles represents an effective and potentially very powerful way to modify American eating habits.

State-wide and community involvement

The involvement of individual states, and community participation, are key components of the *5 A Day* programme. The programme relies heavily on its state and community leaders to put the programme into action.

Within the *5 A Day* programme, state health agencies are licensed by the NCI to coordinate *5 A Day* activities at the state level. States are encouraged to develop coalitions as a forum for collaboration between the public and private sectors. State *5 A Day* coalitions include representatives from state and local government, the fruit and vegetable industry, commodity boards/commissions, farmers' markets, food assistance programmes, professional and voluntary organisations, community groups, medical centres, schools, universities, media outlets and business. The structure and composition of these coalitions are left to the discretion of the state programme coordinators, so that the programme design can be tailored to meet the needs of each state. The programme guidelines[16] provide a national template for state and local activities.

All recipes, photography, advertising, publicity, and other intervention materials related to the programme follow the same standards and therefore have the potential for being used by partners throughout the country. Furthermore, since all partners agree to participate in at least one promotion a year, a standard is set for a minimum level of promotional activity.

Mass media

Mass media plays an essential role in the national *5 A Day* programme. The media has been found to be more effective in achieving behaviour change when combined with interactive components. Building on the lessons from other community-based trials and using a theory-driven, social marketing approach, the mass media component of the *5 A Day* programme is implemented in a complementary fashion at the national level by NCI's Office of Cancer Communications and by PBH. Focus group research was used to design targeted messages to the programme's primary audience, identified as healthy members of the general public who are currently eating 2-3 servings of fruit and vegetables daily. Routine feedback from consumers, a central concept in the social marketing approach, helps ensure that the *5 A Day* messages maintain their freshness and relevance.

Events held throughout the year promote the *5 A Day* message in the media to the public. These initiatives involve broadcast media, use of national spokespersons, print materials and paid media events. Special *5 A Day* events, such as the World's Largest Fruit Basket, involve the local community and create media interest. Periodic promotional campaigns that focus on specific themes, such as salads, fitness, entertaining, or microwaving, keep the programme fresh and visible in grocery stores. Licensed states are encouraged to adapt these themes to their own state-based interventions. National *5 A Day Week*, held each September, allows all partners to join forces for a period of high visibility, theme-related promotion.

In 1995, the *5 A Day Week* theme of 'Take the *5 A Day* Challenge' aimed to move consumers beyond awareness towards behaviour change. Media efforts urged state or local opinion leaders such as athletes, disc jockeys, politicians and other celebrities to have fun and challenge each other to eat five servings each day for a week. The challenge was issued to the public nationally by astronauts using contemporary communications technology, in this case via a video news release transmitted by a satellite to television outlets across the nation.

Theoretical underpinnings

Theoretical models play an important role in developing the interventions, strategies, and media messages used at the national and state levels and in designing an outcome evaluation. Most of the theoretical models used have also been applied in varying degrees in the cardiovascular disease community trials and programmes.

The specific objectives of the *5 A Day* programme are:

- to enhance public awareness of the need to eat five or more servings of fruits and vegetables daily and

- to effect positive dietary behaviour change.

In employing strategies that build consumer skills, provide social support, and make the structural changes necessary to create positive dietary behaviour, a framework is established within the *5 A Day* programme to move beyond a public awareness campaign to improving the eating habits of Americans.

Programme communications are designed to recognise that people will be at different points in their readiness to act on the *5 A Day* message:

- some people will be unaware of the message or aware of it but not yet ready to take action;

- some will be at the point of planning or acting upon the message;

- some will be looking for ways to maintain the behaviour of eating five fruits and vegetables or more daily.

To reach these multiple segments that are at different points in the behaviour change process, the programme encourages partners to use a mix of both awareness and skills-building activities. This concept of behaviour change as a stage-based process is drawn from the Stages of Change or Transtheoretical Model,[17, 18] and provides an overall framework for guiding the translation of *5 A Day* programming until the end of the decade.

Stimulating awareness among Americans of the need to increase fruit and vegetable intake is a first step in promoting the *5 A Day* message. The awareness construct, a cornerstone of the communication-persuasion approaches, is recognised as an important mediating variable between the acquisition of new knowledge and behaviour change.[19, 20] Motivation is also an important pre-requisite to stimulating healthy behaviour change. Drawing on theories of persuasion, for example Consumer Information Processing proposed by McGuire,[19] many of the messages developed within the *5 A Day* programme are designed to motivate, in addition to creating awareness and enhancing knowledge. Giving people lots of reasons to change, some of which are based on perceived relationships between fruit and vegetable consumption and immediate and long-term health risks and perceived benefits of and barriers to eating more fruits and vegetables, constructs drawn from the Health Belief Model,[21, 22] helps to inform convincing and timely *5 A Day* messages and strategies.

Once people are aware, interested, and motivated to change their eating behaviour, they are ready to attend to the more action-oriented or interactive components of behavioural change. Key components drawn from the Social Learning Theory[23, 24] for getting people involved in the behavioural change process include: raising self-efficacy through skills-building information and positive modelling prior to making choices; triggering behaviour change by providing cues to reinforce the message at point of sale; and encouraging more supportive normative behaviour within media, peer, family, community, and food purchasing environments. These components, applied to *5 A Day* intervention strategies, provide the vehicles for successful behaviour change. An additional construct, taken from the Social Learning Theory and applied to the *5 A Day* programme, is modifying the environmental setting, for example in workplace cafeterias, supermarkets or restaurants, in order to support dietary behaviour change.

Thus, within the *5 A Day* programme, the theoretical framework – or template – for dietary behaviour change is established at the national level and is put into operation at the state level. Working closely with the state licensees, the programme encourages them to apply these theoretical approaches in the design and evaluation of their intervention efforts.

Channels

Channels such as schools, supermarkets, workplaces, churches, food assistance programmes, restaurants, and civic and service organisations are a valuable organising tool for community interventions and provide consistency in the delivery of *5 A Day* messages and scientifically-based activities to millions of consumers. These channels can provide both educational opportunities and increased access to healthy foods. Channels are also open systems, interfacing with the larger community at a number of points, and thus providing opportunities for changing social norms. Three commonly used channels are supermarkets, schools and workplaces.

Supermarkets

Nutrition interventions in supermarkets have the potential of reaching consumers in all demographic strata. Supermarkets were the first channel to be used in the *5 A Day* programme and are the channel which has received the most attention, including the use of the *5 A Day* theme and logo in print and broadcast advertisements. The programme encourages supermarkets to organise interactive events, such as supermarket tours and taste tests, to attract the attention of consumers and engage them. For example, the Dole Food Company Supermarket Tours Project, which provides store tours for school children and features the *5 A Day* message, is currently in use among a large number of schools across the US. In this way, supermarkets can also serve as a medium for cross-channel activity.

Schools

Schools are one of the channels most frequently used as a setting for *5 A Day* interventions. *5 A Day* school-based interventions often consist of either classroom or cafeteria activities. In encouraging a combination of both types of activities, the programme provides an opportunity both to enhance knowledge and awareness of the *5 A Day* message within the classroom and to increase the visibility and availability of fruits and vegetables in the cafeteria. Four of the nine NCI *5 A Day* grants include school-based interventions that incorporate classroom and cafeteria components, as well as parental involvement.[25] Several state agencies and industry partners have also developed different curricula for use in schools and have designed and implemented various school activities.

Workplaces

Workplaces are another frequently used channel. This setting offers access to a substantial proportion of the adult population and includes social support systems to assist individuals in changing their behaviour. In *5 A Day*, states are spreading the *5 A Day* message in workplaces by means of inserts in wage packets and workplace health programmes. Three of the nine NCI *5 A Day* research grants are also conducting workplace-based interventions involving networks of peer educational programmes and family support in changing eating habits in the workplace.

Research and evaluation

The *5 A Day* programme combines research with a national health promotion programme. Its research strategy differs from the first generation of community trials in two ways. Firstly, the intervention addresses a single, simple nutrition message. Secondly, the research is focused in specific community channels to allow for random assignment of large sample sizes (n=12 to 24 community channels), a design which provides more power than the community-wide trials. This design will also produce tested interventions for a variety of settings which can be combined into a community-wide or national effort.

Both intervention research and nationwide evaluation are well under way. The research component consists of nine community-based research studies, funded in 1993 for four years by NCI.[25] The purpose of these grants is to implement and evaluate interventions aimed at increasing fruit and vegetable consumption among specific population segments in particular community channels, including workplaces, schools, churches, and food assistance programmes.[25]

The NCI, with assistance from PBH, conducted a national survey to measure consumption in 1996 and a process evaluation of intervention activities by states. The NCI also funded, in 1994 and 1995, in coordination with the national Centers for Disease Control (CDC), eight grants to evaluate *5 A Day* activities implemented at the state level within specific community channels. In 1994 and 1995, CDC funded more than 30 intervention grants for one year addressing *5 A Day* project areas.

Results of the survey on consumption and results from the nine channel-specific research grants will provide more data for future programme directions.

Summary and conclusion

The *5 A Day* programme is a national public/private partnership which aims to encourage Americans to eat five or more servings of fruit and vegetables daily. Distinguishing features of the National *5 A Day* programme are:

- the activation of government and food industry systems at national, state and local levels

- the creation of public/private and national/state/local partnerships

- the development of periodic and theme-related mass media

- the generation of activity in organised channels that reaches the public directly, and

- the use of channel-specific interventions.

References

1   Doll R, Peto R. 1981. The causes of cancer: quantitative estimates of avoidable risk of cancer in the United States today. *Journal of the National Cancer Institute*; 66: 1191–1308.

2   US Department of Health and Human Services. Greenwald P, Sondik E (eds). 1986. *Cancer Control Objectives for the Nation: 1985–2000.* National Cancer Institute Monograph (2). Rockville, Maryland: Department of Health and Human Services.

3   US Department of Health and Human Services, Public Health Service. 1988. *The Surgeon General's Report on Nutrition and Health.* Washington DC: Government Printing Office.

4   National Academy of Sciences. 1989. *Diet and Health: Implications for Reducing Chronic Disease Risk.* Washington DC: National Academy Press.

5   US Department of Health and Human Services. 1990. *Healthy People 2000: National Health Promotion and Disease Prevention Objectives.* DHHS Pub. No. (PHS) 91–50212. Washington DC: Government Printing Office.

6   US Departments of Agriculture and Health and Human Services. 1995. *Nutrition and Your Health: Dietary Guidelines for Americans.* Home and Garden Bulletin No. 232. Washington DC: US Departments of Agriculture and Health and Human Services.

7   Steinmetz KA, Potter JD. 1991. Vegetables, fruit, and cancer. I. Epidemiology. *Cancer Causes and Control*; 2: 325–357.

8   Block G, Patterson B, Subar A. 1992. Fruit, vegetables, and cancer prevention: A review of the epidemiological evidence. *Nutrition and Cancer*; 18: 1–29.

9   Ziegler RG. 1991. Vegetables, fruits, and carotenoids and the risk of cancer. *American Journal of Clinical Nutrition*; 53: 251S–259S.

10 Ziegler RG et al. 1992. Does beta carotene explain why reduced cancer risk is associated with vegetable and fruit intake? *Cancer Research*: 2060S–2066S.

11 Negri E et al. 1991. Vegetable and fruit consumption and cancer risk. *International Journal of Cancer*; 48: 350–354.

12 Willett WC. 1990. Vitamin A and lung cancer. *Nutrition Review*; 48: 5: 201–211.

13 Steinmetz KA, Potter JD. 1991. Vegetables, fruit, and cancer. II. Mechanisms. *Cancer Causes and Control*; 2: 427–441.

14 Heimendinger J et al. 1996. The National 5-A-Day for Better Health Program: A large scale nutrition intervention. *Journal of Public Health Management Practice*; 2: 2: 27–35.

15 Foerster SB et al. 1995. California's Five a Day – for Better Health! campaign: An innovative population-based effort to effect large-scale dietary change. *American Journal of Preventive Medicine*; 11: 2: 124–131.

16 National Cancer Institute. 1994. *5 A Day for Better Health Program. Program Guidebook.* Bethesda, Maryland: National Cancer Institute.

17 Prochaska JO, DiClemente CC. 1992. Stages of change in the modification of problem behaviors. In: Hersen M, Eisler RM, Millers PM (eds). *Progress in Behavior Modification.* New York: Academic Press.

18 Prochaska JO, DiClemente CC. 1982. Transtheoretical therapy: Toward a more integrative model of change. *Psychotherapy: Theory, Research, and Practice*; 20: 161–173.

19 McGuire WJ. 1985. Attitudes and attitude change. In: Lindzey G, Aronsen E (eds). *Handbook of Social Psychology,* vol 2, third edition. New York: Random House.

20 Cialdini RB, Petty RE, Cacioppo JT. 1981. Attitude and attitude change. *Annual Reviews in Psychology*; 32: 357–404.

21 Janz ND, Becker MH. 1984. *The Health Belief Model: A Decade Later.* Health Education Monographs 11: 1–47.

22 Rosenstock IM. 1990. The Health Belief Model: Explaining health behavior through expectancies. In: Glanz K, Lewis RM, Rimer BK (eds). *Health Behavior and Health Education: Theory, Research and Practice.* San Francisco: Jossey-Bass.

23 Bandura A. 1977. *Social Learning Theory.* Englewood Cliffs, New Jersey: Prentice-Hall.

24 Glanz K, Lewis FM, Rimer BK. 1990. *Health Behavior and Health Education: Theory, Research and Practice.* San Francisco: Jossey-Bass.

25 Havas S et al. 1994. 5 A Day for Better Health: A new research initiative. *Journal of the American Dietetic Association*; 94: 32–36.

Chapter 9

The *Get Fresh* campaign

Bill Bowman

Fresh Produce Consortium

Carole Stewart

Hammond Communications Ltd

Introduction

"Sex, food, drink, exercise and sunshine are all covered by an increasing number of public health warnings – but the government agency that issues them has found itself facing revolt from a public bored by perpetual nagging." *Sunday Times, 3 March 1996*[1]

"Most campaigns don't work when you are driving people in the opposite direction from the one they want to go in." *Chief Executive of the Association for Public Health*[1]

This is the climate in which the Fresh Produce Consortium decided to develop a campaign to increase consumption of fresh vegetables and fruit in the UK. The £500,000 generic campaign, funded by companies and associations operating in the industry, was launched in March 1996 under the banner 'Get Fresh'.

In order to develop the campaign, a wide range of published data was assessed and further research was undertaken with the aim of analysing how consumers thought and felt, and which approaches they responded to best. The analysis was based not on demographics, but on psychographics, also known as TGI (Target Group Index) cluster analysis. This is a national database linking grocery spending, attitudes, lifestyle and exposure to different forms of media (press, TV and so on). The analysis is statistically very robust and very useful in guiding marketing activity.

The Apathetics and the Foodies: the target groups for the campaign

Five consumer clusters in the fresh fruit and vegetable sector were identified. These were described as: Traditionalists, Apathetics, Demi-Veggies, Couch Potatoes and Foodies. Two of those groups, the Foodies and the Apathetics, were identified as the target groups for at least the first year of the campaign.

The rationale for selecting those two groups was that they not only included the highest proportion of individuals, but also showed the greatest volume of opportunity if the way they thought and behaved about food could be changed (see Table 1). Focusing on two groups was likely to achieve more than spreading activity thinly across all consumers.

Table 1   *Potential target groups for the campaign*

	Number of households	Number of individuals	£ value of fresh fruit market	£ value of fresh vegetables market
Traditionalists	21%	18%	22%	22%
Apathetics	21%	23%	18%	18%
Demi-Veggies	18%	16%	20%	19%
Couch Potatoes	19%	17%	14%	15%
Foodies	21%	25%	26%	26%

The Apathetics were the focus for much of the early activity of the campaign. They tend to be younger mothers and fathers in the C1, C2 and D groups, aged between 18 and 44, who are buying for larger households, generally of four or more people. They are currently under-performing in the purchase of fresh vegetables and fruit. Their apathy is a function of habit or convenience rather than outright rejection. This group therefore offers the opportunity of increasing the market for fresh staples and affordable exotica.

The second main target group was the Foodies. They already represent the largest single share of the total value of the fruit and vegetable market (26%), yet their per capita spending is low relative to their receptivity. They are already sensitised to issues of healthy diet and food quality, have a relatively high purchasing power and are willing to experiment, thus offering opportunities for out-of-season and exotic produce. Foodies tend to be mid- to up-market working mothers in the B, C1 and C2 groups, aged between 25 and 54, and living in households of three or more.

Attitudes to fresh vegetables and fruit

Having identified the target groups, a logo and slogan were developed (see above). Focus groups of Apathetics and Foodies were set up to explore current attitudes to fresh vegetables and fruit and to gauge levels of awareness and attitudes to previous campaigns. A summary of the reactions of the Apathetics is given in Table 2.

Table 2 *Attitudes of the Apathetics to fresh vegetables and fruit*

Attitudes to fresh vegetables
Frozen is perceived as nutritionally just as good and much more practical
Fresh is seen as expensive, wasteful and generally a nuisance (for something as dull as vegetables)

Attitudes to fresh fruit
Mixed feelings: appetising, juicy and colourful but expensive, boring and fiddly
Highly seasonal: ie for summer
Tinned fruit, especially with cream, is seen as an acceptable alternative

Most of the people in the Apathetics group are working mothers with little time or inclination to cook. Convenience is absolutely vital to them and they could not survive without their freezers. Their children are allowed to eat more or less what they want. The Apathetics are not motivated by traditional health messages; indeed they are resentful and dismissive of them.

There was some residual awareness of an 'eat five a day' campaign, which the Apathetics rejected as being too demanding and restrictive, and essentially about denial. There were comments such as "Five portions every day of fruit – you'd have to be a vegetarian to have all that."

The Apathetics were also asked their views on the proposition of fresh fruit and vegetables as an 'enjoyable diet'. This was a difficult concept for Apathetics to accept. (Even the Foodies felt it was a dull and worthy approach.) The Apathetics saw consumption of fruit and vegetables as a link to slimming diets rather than to general well-being and health. They also felt strongly that consumption of fruit and vegetables was about denial, or perhaps even 'punishment' eating.

The issue of fruit and vegetables as the way to a 'healthier lifestyle' was discussed. This was of genuine interest, particularly to those concerned with family health. However, the secondary benefits of better health (better quality of life, better skin, better fitness, and better sex life) were considered more motivating than longer life.

The Apathetics recognised that there is probably value in eating fresh vegetables and fruit, but do not currently feel compelled to do anything about it. In the words of one of the respondents: "Someone's going to have to brainwash me to make me and my kids eat more fruit and vegetables."

Finally, their reaction to the logo and slogan was tested. These were seen as positive, snappy, energetic and witty; the *double entendre* was well liked by most, and recognised immediately as less 'worthy' than other approaches.

The first year of the campaign

The first year of the *Get Fresh* campaign had three main elements: the Get Fresh Show, Search for a Get Fresh Star, and the use of celebrities.

The Get Fresh Show is a totally new concept in Britain, but one which has been very successful in the United States. It is a comedy roadshow that played to live audiences throughout the UK, linking up with media partners on the way. The show, which starred an up-and-coming comedian with appeal to the Apathetic audience, took a witty, irreverent look at modern living, debunking the many myths about what people should and should not eat and drink. It used humour to pass on some very basic guidelines, in a very palatable form, about how to eat and exercise sensibly in order to get more out of life. It got across a clear message about fresh fruit and vegetables, but in a totally unworthy and 'unpreachy' way. The belief was that this was the best way to get the message across to a section of the public more in tune with *Baywatch* and the Lottery than experimental recipes and cholesterol.

At the end of the roadshow tour, the Search for a Get Fresh Star was launched. This is a tried, tested, but not tired method of directly involving the public and generating media coverage – not in the up-market women's magazines that devote acres of excellent copy to fruit and vegetables already, but in the type of media devoured by the target audience for the campaign.

Celebrities from popular 'soaps' and from the world of sports and music with particular appeal to the target audiences were identified. A few interviews in the right media focusing on the individual celebrity's physical stamina, looks, or health and attributing them to fruit and vegetables and physical activity does more to develop street credibility for fresh produce than 100,000 leaflets on healthy eating.

Telling a working class 24 year old man or woman to eat more fresh produce because it will help reduce the chances of heart disease in later life will not be successful. For these people later life is light years away. But telling them they will have better skin, look better on the beach, play better football or have a better sex life will get their attention.

Reference

1   Rogers L. 1996. Choking on our health warnings. *Sunday Times: 3 March 1996.*

Chapter 10

The role of the media

Peter Bazalgette

Bazal Productions

The media can play an important role in encouraging people to eat more fruit and vegetables. However, three points need to be made:

1   The media can be positive but will be, and should be, sceptical.

Health messages change over time. For example, dietary advice 20 years ago would have included cutting down on red wine and oily fish as ways of reducing the risk of heart disease. The role of food in heart disease has been emphasised in the past two decades, and the importance of physical activity underplayed. Advice in ten years' time may not be identical to current advice and therefore the media is liable to remain sceptical about whether health messages are for today, or for today and tomorrow.

One major change since the 1980s is that health messages are now positive messages about what people can and ought to do rather than negative messages about what they should not do. Positive messages are easier for the media to put across.

2   The media should not be boring.

Healthy eating is a boring term and can be a turn-off for many people. As a feature on the *Food and Drink Programme*, four advertising companies were asked to devise an advertisement, aimed at 11–14 year old children, giving a positive message about either oranges or brown bread. The four companies independently came up with the same rationale, choosing not to give a straight healthy eating message as they believed that children would find this boring. Instead their advertisements emphasised the fun and fashionable aspects, and appealed to children's sense of humour. People need to be enthused to eat good food, largely on the basis that it is enjoyable.

3   The media need to encourage and enable, without being didactic.

Young people no longer learn cooking skills either at school or at home, and many adults lack cooking skills too. The media has an important role to play in giving people those cooking skills.

Food game shows have proved to be very popular. In *Ready, Steady, Cook*, two members of the audience present a bag of ingredients and challenge chefs to make a dish with them. In 1996 it was the second most popular daytime programme. Audience research indicates that the programme is particularly popular among students, and that viewers perceive it as a cookery show rather than a game show. In *Can't Cook, Won't Cook*, which is televised every morning, people who say they 'can't cook' or 'won't cook' are nominated by their partner and cook a dish on the programme, with help from the chef presenter. The popularity of both these programmes indicates the demand for learning cooking skills.

Many people find fruit and vegetables boring because they do not know what to do with them or how to make them taste good. The media cannot afford to be boring. By encouraging and enabling people to cook and prepare food through lively and entertaining programmes, the media can play its part in helping to increase consumption of fruit and vegetables in the UK. This is likely to be far more successful than adopting a didactic approach.

Peter Bazalgette is an independent TV producer responsible for the production of about 300 food programmes a year for British television.

Discussion: promoting vegetables and fruit

Consumer interest in food issues

There is a tendency to underestimate public interest in food issues. The large television audience sizes of certain food programmes indicate the high level of public interest.

This interest is confirmed by the experience of food and health writers. The potential impact of the print media is often under-estimated. Consumer interest could be further increased by finding ways of involving readers in issues, possibly through quizzes and surveys.

Consumer perceptions of science and risk

Although the fruit and vegetable message may have remained constant, there remains a public perception that scientists 'change their minds'. Furthermore, several consumer food scares have diminished public confidence in health messages.

The issue of how science is presented is perhaps one of the most crucial current issues. During the BSE crisis, for example, the government provided little information on relative risk. It has also been suggested that the shortfalls in research funding push scientists into presenting extreme versions of their research findings in order to obtain further funding.

It is important to develop a way of improving public understanding of risk assessment and of increasing awareness that science does move on. The media could play an important role in getting these messages across. There may be a role for a quasi-government agency which draws on risk experts from all the British universities and acts as a consumer clearing house for scientific messages. In parallel with this, the medical journals could include commentaries on research findings, including the implications for public health strategies.

Health claims and consumer confidence

There is concern that current legislation does not allow manufacturers or retailers of fruit and vegetables to promote the potential health benefits of those products. It is possible that new legislation or government advice on health claims could relax these restrictions. However, any criteria for judging health claims need to be reliable so that consumers can have complete confidence in any claims which are made. Any spurious claims are only likely to lower consumer confidence further and possibly damage the overall message relating to fruit and vegetables.

Nutrition education for health professionals

The nutrition education of health professionals needs to be improved. Following Health of the Nation initiatives in England and similar initiatives in other parts of the UK, considerable progress has been made and the mechanisms for nutrition education for professionals have been put in place. They now need to be implemented.

Nutrition education in schools

The school curriculum needs to devote more time to practical food skills. The areas relating to food in the current curriculum are largely theoretical rather than practical.

Nutrition education for trainee teachers also needs to be improved. A survey of the nutrition knowledge of student teachers found that very few could name any sources of many nutrients – for example, only 3% could name any source of folic acid.[1]

Resources for industry initiatives

In 1996, the Fresh Produce Consortium (FPC) launched *Get Fresh*, a marketing initiative designed to increase consumption of fresh fruit and vegetables. While there is recognition of the FPC's achievement in obtaining funding for this campaign, the initiative, like others, has suffered from a shortage of cash.

One possible source of additional funding for initiatives to promote fruit and vegetables in cooperation with partners in other Member States, is the European Union, through the Commission's health education programme. The FPC has already explored this.

National government support

Strong leadership from government is essential for the successful promotion of fruit and vegetables in the UK. This may include a strategic role, communication of the message, and alliance building.

The government provided much support and leadership by establishing the Nutrition Task Force and the Scottish Diet Action Group. The Nutrition Task Force Product Promotion Project Team proposed a high profile government-led and funded public information campaign to encourage increased consumption of fruit and vegetables as well as bread, pasta, rice and other cereal products, potatoes and fish. However, the government rejected the proposal, stating that: "It is for the relevant sectors to grasp the marketing opportunities presented by the quest for healthy eating to promote their products to the public."

The demise of the Task Force does not mean that there is no longer a need for continued leadership from government. Although producers are committed to taking action to increase fruit and vegetable consumption, they are more likely to fund such initiatives if the government is prepared to take a lead.

The Department of Health and the Ministry of Agriculture, Fisheries and Food are keen to offer cooperation and support in ways other than simply providing funding. For example, the resources which have been provided for the Nutrition Task Force, in terms of support and secretariat, remain. They are also keen to encourage alliance building. The national Nutrition Task Force and the Scottish Diet Action Group have both placed a heavy emphasis on alliances from the community taking the lead. However, while local alliances are important, they are not enough on their own.

The Ministry of Agriculture, Fisheries and Food also has a role in dissemination of research. It funds much research on basic nutrition, including the Food Choice and Acceptability research programme which has looked, for example, at how to overcome the barriers to increased fruit and vegetable consumption. There is a need to ensure that the results of this programme are widely disseminated.

Mechanisms for change

Consideration of the options for change at a policy and regulatory level need to include the mechanisms for change. To address some of the concerns around public health, an alternative structure may be required, perhaps in the form of an independent Food Standards Agency. Alternatively, a National Food Policy Council might coordinate the disparate messages from different agencies. Further debate on this issue is needed to work out the best mechanism in terms of consumer protection and public health.

Reference

1   Sanderson M. 1996. Personal communication.

Ideas for action

Introduction

There was strong support at the National Heart Forum expert meeting for a national coordinated and sustained strategy to increase vegetable and fruit consumption. Such a strategy should tackle availability and access to vegetables and fruit as well as changing attitudes and awareness. It should include a high profile information campaign and be supported by structural change and local action.

The government, all sections of the food industry (producers, processors and manufacturers, retailers and caterers), health authorities and health professionals, local authorities, schools, the media and advertisers, the voluntary sector, consumer groups, and researchers and academics, all need to be involved in developing and implementing the strategy.

One option would be for a national coalition, funded by government, industry and other stakeholders, such as health groups. The government, particularly the Department of Health and Ministry of Agriculture, Fisheries and Food, could take a strategic lead in promoting vegetable and fruit consumption, by ensuring that the various players are brought together to establish a sustained multi-sectoral strategy, including a national 'At Least Five a Day' campaign, with perhaps a national promotional day, and by funding initiatives to kick start the national information campaign. The government also has a role in coordinating research and disseminating findings. (See also Chapter 1.)

Much can be done at the European Union level too. It is important that the 1996 reforms of the fruit and vegetables regime of the Common Agricultural Policy are implemented in the UK in such a way as to increase vegetable and fruit consumption. It is important, however, that the fruit and vegetables regime of the CAP is not considered in isolation. The effect of the CAP on the relative pricing of other products also impacts on fruit and vegetable consumption and needs to be examined (see page 43). Article 129 of the Maastricht Treaty, which establishes a protocol for public health input into policy, can be used to ensure that European policies do not hinder an increase in fruit and vegetable consumption. There may be a role for a European Nutrition Council to promote consideration of nutrition issues in European Union policy.

In the UK, there are many ways in which the various sectors can help contribute to an increase in vegetable and fruit consumption. The following pages offer a selection of ideas for action, which emerged from the National Heart Forum expert meeting.

THE FOOD INDUSTRY

Farmers and growers

- Consider expanding the remit of the Horticultural Development Council (HDC) to cover promotional and educational activities.

- Growers to reassess British growing patterns against current and future eating patterns. The British growing industry should take advantage of the huge potential offered by an increase in vegetable and fruit consumption by changing growing patterns where appropriate.

- Find ways of promoting traditional British produce in ways which fit into modern lives.

- Distribute surplus fruit and vegetables to schools and nurseries.

- Improve links between growers and consumers, so that growers can become more responsive to changes in demand. Options such as farmers' markets and local box schemes, where produce is supplied directly to consumers, may help.

- The HDC or other bodies of growers should monitor food advertising to ensure that adverts do not contravene the Code of Advertising Practice by discouraging fruit and vegetable consumption. Potential offenders should be reported to the Advertising Standards Authority.

- Growers to invest in their responsibility for marketing, to help increase promotion of vegetables and fruit.

- Growers to act collectively to seek funding from the European Union to promote fruit and vegetables.

Food retailers

- Develop new and innovative ways to promote vegetables and fruit. This could include:
  - producing and distributing leaflets about vegetables and fruit
  - organising in-store cookery demonstrations
  - setting up tasting sessions
  - recipe promotions, linking ingredients and recipes
  - special pricing offers on vegetables and fruit.

- Make use of Electronic Point of Sale data for research on fruit and vegetable consumption patterns and on the impact of any promotional or educational interventions.

- Explore ways of improving local access to vegetables and fruit, particularly in areas where availability of fresh vegetables and fruit is currently a problem. This could include:
  - mobile shopping facilities
  - free or subsidised transport schemes for consumers to get to and from stores
  - telephone ordering and delivery service
  - collaboration with local initiatives, such as co-operatives.

- Improve local supply systems by working more closely with local growers.

- Fast food retailers to sell foods rich in vegetables and fruit.

- Supermarkets to display fruit at checkouts.

Caterers and food manufacturers

- Place more emphasis on promotion of vegetables and fruit, and dishes containing them.

- Incorporate extra fruit and vegetables as ingredients in familiar dishes.

- Promote unusual fruit and vegetables or imaginative serving ideas.

- Use price incentives and pricing strategies to encourage consumption of vegetables and fruit, for example by including vegetables or a side salad in the price of the meal.

- Introduce a variety of healthy snacks, such as fruit and fruit juice, into vending machines in schools and workplaces.

- Adapt healthy eating initiatives, such as the HeartBeat Award scheme, to promote vegetables and fruit.

- Specify in catering contracts the amount of fruit and vegetable provision in every meal. Guidelines, such the Scottish Diet Action Group's guidelines on public sector catering, could be useful in ensuring that this happens.

HEALTH AUTHORITIES AND HEALTH PROFESSIONALS

- Health care purchasers, providers and health professionals to take a lead in establishing local alliances to increase vegetable and fruit consumption, particularly among children and low income consumers.

- Directors of Public Health to use their annual reports to review the availability of and access to vegetables and fruit.

- Health promotion departments to conduct audits of local facilities to ensure that vegetables and fruit are readily accessible and promoted.

- Work with retailers, including supermarkets, on promotional campaigns to increase fruit and vegetable consumption.

- Dietitians to offer training to caterers to encourage them to use vegetables and fruit.

- Health authorities to evaluate initiatives to increase fruit and vegetable consumption and disseminate examples of good practice and effective interventions.

- Health professionals such as GPs, nurses, midwives and health visitors to promote the 'at least five a day' message when giving dietary advice.

- Professionals to receive training, at basic, post-basic and in-service levels, in nutrition and in health promotion theory and techniques. Nutrition training should emphasise the health benefits of vegetables and fruit.

LOCAL AUTHORITIES

- Work with health authorities to establish local alliances to promote consumption of vegetables and fruit, with a particular focus on children and low income consumers.

- Promote consumption of vegetables and fruit within public sector catering, eg social services and school meals.

- Use planning powers to ensure that there is wide access to affordable vegetables and fruit, by encouraging street markets and through decisions on retail outlets and store siting.

- Support community-based initiatives such as co-operatives, community horticulture, box schemes, community cafés and food coupon schemes.

SCHOOLS

- Introduce school food policies which help promote consumption of vegetables and fruit among children.

- Ensure that school meals contracts specify, for example, how many portions of vegetables and fruit are to be included in school meals, and that they are monitored.

- Explore novel and imaginative techniques to promote fruit and vegetables in schools. These could include:
  - breakfast clubs
  - 'fruit only' breaks
  - healthy tuckshop initiatives, including selling fruit in school tuckshops, and including fruit in vending machines
  - mobile fruit vans
  - school horticulture projects
  - headteachers and teachers encouraging parents to include fruit in their children's packed lunches
  - taste tests to introduce pupils to new fruit and vegetables both in school meals and tuckshops
  - Smart Card schemes or other schemes which reward fruit and vegetable choices
  - collaboration with local growers or retailers to explore provision of free or subsidised fruit.

- Education departments, schools and curriculum advisory bodies to strengthen the teaching of nutrition and cooking skills in schools.

MEDIA AND ADVERTISERS

- Advertising agencies to devise and disseminate ideas to improve the image of fruit and vegetables by portraying them as tasty, fun, interesting, convenient and easy to prepare.

- Recipes in women's magazines to include more fruit and vegetables.

- Good food awards to focus one year on the best and most imaginative promotion of fruit and vegetables.

VOLUNTARY SECTOR/CONSUMER GROUPS

- Heart and cancer charities to promote the 'Eat at least five a day' message. Options include:
    - information packs on the benefits of vegetables and fruit
    - help in organising in-store promotions and demonstrations
    - collaborating with industry in innovative ways to promote the message and products.

- Consumer groups to use their credibility to promote the 'Eat at least five a day' message.

- Make *At Least Five A Day* a national campaign

- Introduce an award scheme for the best catering initiative promoting fruit and vegetables.

- Provide information for the food industry and consumers on the health benefits of vegetables and fruit, effective interventions, and ways to prepare fruit and vegetables.

- Use celebrities to promote fruit and vegetables and raise awareness.

- Local consumer groups to audit and campaign on local accessibility and availability of fruit and vegetables.

RESEARCHERS AND ACADEMICS

- Evaluate practical national and local interventions to increase fruit and vegetable consumption and widely disseminate information learned about the effectiveness of interventions.

- Carry out a comprehensive review of the effectiveness of interventions to increase fruit and vegetable consumption.

At least five a day. Strategies to increase vegetable and fruit consumption

List of participants

Professor Annie Anderson, School of Management and Consumer Studies, University of Dundee

Ms Xanthe Awaritakis, Cancer Research Campaign

Mr Peter Bazalgette, Bazal Productions

Mr Bill Bowman, Fresh Produce Consortium/Covent Garden Market Authority

Ms Angela Bradley, Health Promotion Agency for Northern Ireland

Mr Andrew Brown, Researcher, Labour Party Agriculture Team

Ms Caroline Brown, Institute of Grocery Distribution

Ms Lynda Brown, Guild of Food Writers

Dr Eric Brunner, Department of Epidemiology and Public Health, University College London

Mr Geoffrey Cannon, National Food Alliance/World Cancer Research Fund

Mr Andrew Carpenter, British Retail Consortium

Ms Gill Cawdron, Administrative Manager, National Heart Forum

Ms Samantha Church, Projects Officer, National Heart Forum

Professor Dame Barbara Clayton, Chair, Health of the Nation Nutrition Task Force

Ms Peta Cottee, National Food Alliance

Dr David Cox, Institute of Food Research

Ms Julie Dallison, Maternity Alliance

Mr John Davis, Local Authority Caterers Association

Mr Stephen Dornan, Scottish Federation of Community Food Initiatives

Ms Liz Dowler, Human Nutrition Unit, London School of Hygiene and Tropical Medicine

Ms Pauline Doyle, Policy Communications Officer, National Heart Forum

Ms Jane Eaton, British Dietetic Association

Mr Ian Finlandson, Department of Health

Ms Ann Foster, Scottish Consumer Council

Dr Godfrey Fowler, Royal College of General Practitioners

Ms Alice Furniss, Food Commission

Mr Nigel Garbutt, Safeway Stores plc

Dr Richard Harding, Consumers and Nutrition Policy Division, Ministry of
Agriculture, Fisheries and Food

Mr Trevor Hayes, National Farmers Union

Mr D Henderson, Fresh Produce Consortium

Mr Spencer Henson, Department of Agriculture and Economics, University of
Reading

Ms Pat Hindley, Fresh Fruit and Vegetable Information Bureau

Ms Deirdre Hutton, Scottish Consumer Council

Ms Jill Johnstone, National Consumer Council

Professor Desmond Julian, Chair, National Heart Forum

Mr Damien Killeen, Scottish Food Poverty Alliance

Ms Jean King, Cancer Research Campaign

Professor Tim Lang, Centre for Food Policy, Thames Valley University

Professor Mike Lean, Department of Human Nutrition, Glasgow Royal
Infirmary

Ms Suzi Leather, Food Policy Consultant

Ms Rosie Leyden, Wordworks

Professor Alan Malcolm, Institute of Food Research

Dr Alan Maryon Davis, Faculty of Public Health Medicine

Ms Karen McColl, Consultant

Ms Diane McCrea, Consumers' Association

Ms Norma McGough, British Diabetic Association

Professor A J McMichael, Department of Epidemiology and Population
Sciences, London School of Hygiene and Tropical Medicine

Professor Anne Murcott, 'The Nation's Diet,' South Bank University

Dr Noel Olsen, British Medical Association

Ms Claire Paisley, Health Promotion Wales

Ms Dilwen Phillips, National Federation of Women's Institutes

Ms Dawn Porter, Northern Ireland Chest, Heart and Stroke Association

Mr Derek Ray, Department of Agricultural Economics, Wye College

Dr Mike Rayner, Department of Public Health and Primary Care, University of
Oxford

Lord Rea, Individual Member, National Heart Forum

Ms Maeve Robertson, Member, MAFF Consumer Panel

Ms Sallie Robins, British Medical Association

Dr Lesley Rogers, Assistant Director, National Heart Forum

Mr Jim Ryan, Trades Union Congress

Ms Maggie Sanderson, British Dietetic Association/Honorary Secretary,
National Heart Forum

Mr Michael Scott, National Farmers Union/Elgro

Ms Seroj Shah, Health Visitors' Association

Ms Imogen Sharp, Director, National Heart Forum

Professor Prakesh Shetty, Human Nutrition Unit, London School of Hygiene
and Tropical Medicine

Mr Colin Spencer, Guild of Food Writers

Ms Gloria Stables, 5 A Day Program, National Cancer Institute, United States

Ms Sarah Stacey, Guild of Health Writers

Ms Martine Standish, Society of Health Education and Health Promotion
Specialists

Ms Carole Stewart, Hammond Communications Ltd

Ms Lynn Stockley, Health Education Authority

Ms Carmen Taboas, National Consumer Council
Dr Paul Tromans, Welsh Office
Ms Rhiannon Walters, Faculty of Public Health Medicine
Ms Heather Waring, British Heart Foundation
Ms Jane Watkins, Royal Society of Health
Ms Jenni White, Meeting Administrator, National Heart Forum
Dr Michael Wilkinson, Coronary Prevention Group
Ms Carol Williams, Nutrition Consultant
Ms Jill Wordley, Consumers and Nutrition Policy Division, Ministry of
    Agriculture, Fisheries and Food

Observer
Dr Sue Martin, Department of Health

Printed in the United Kingdom for The Stationery Office
Dd303142 3/97 C15 G559 10170